PRIVATISATION OF MIGRATION CONTROL

STUDIES IN LAW, POLITICS, AND SOCIETY

Recent Volumes:

Volumes 1–2:	Edited by Rita J. Simon
Volume 3:	Edited by Steven Spitzer
Volumes 4–9:	Edited by Steven Spitzer and Andrew S. Scull
Volumes 10–16:	Edited by Susan S. Sibey and Austin Sarat
Volumes 17–33:	Edited by Austin Sarat and Patricia Ewick
Volumes 34–77:	Edited by Austin Sarat
Volume 78:	Edited by Livia Holden and Austin Sarat
Volume 79:	Edited by Austin Sarat
Volume 80:	Edited by Austin Sarat
Volume 81:	Edited by Austin Sarat
Volume 82:	Edited by Austin Sarat
Volume 83:	Edited by Austin Sarat
Volume 84:	Edited by Austin Sarat
Volume 85:	Edited by Austin Sarat
Volume 86A:	Edited by Austin Sarat

STUDIES IN LAW, POLITICS, AND SOCIETY VOLUME 86B

PRIVATISATION OF MIGRATION CONTROL: POWER WITHOUT ACCOUNTABILITY?

EDITED BY

AUSTIN SARAT, EDITOR
Amherst College, USA

GUEST EDITED BY

DEVYANI PRABHAT
University of Bristol Law School, UK

emerald PUBLISHING

United Kingdom – North America – Japan
India – Malaysia – China

Emerald Publishing Limited
Emerald Publishing, Floor 5, Northspring, 21-23 Wellington Street, Leeds LS1 4DL.

First edition 2021

British Library Cataloguing in Publication Data
A catalogue record for this book is available from the British Library

ISBN: 978-1-80117-663-7 (Print)
ISBN: 978-1-80117-662-0 (Online)
ISBN: 978-1-80117-664-4 (Epub)

ISSN: 1059-4337 (Series)

Printed and bound by CPI Group (UK) Ltd, Croydon, CR0 4YY

CONTENTS

LIST OF CONTRIBUTORS

Isabella Bertolini	University of Bristol, Law School, UK
Emily Rigler Gillingham	University of Bristol, Law School, UK
Isobel Kamber	University of Bristol, Law School, UK
Akosua-Rose Oppon	University of Bristol, Law School, UK
Harriet Parfitt	University of Bristol, Law School, UK
Devyani Prabhat	University of Bristol, Law School, UK
Aleksandra Wegera	University of Bristol, Law School, UK

EDITORIAL BOARD

INTRODUCTION

Devyani Prabhat

This special issue is the second part of a two-part edited collection on the privatisation of migration. In Part 1, we have analysed the conceptual framework for understanding private participation in immigration control in the UK. There are clear links with national security concerns but these are always necessary for heightened immigration control. In the ordinary and everyday situations as well it is possible to engage in pervasive immigration control. Since 2010 the UK government has increased internal immigration controls by involving private individuals who control access to essential resources like health care, travel, housing, and employment. Individuals such as employers, landlords and medical professionals have been given incentives to report on immigration status as well as threatened with sanctions in case of failure to report immigration status of those whom they come in contact with during the course of their work or lives. Such practices have created fractures in British society and set up internal borders. The resulting atmosphere of hostility towards irregular migrants was initially termed the 'hostile environment'. Following news-stories of wrongful deportations of people who had the right to remain in the UK, such as in the Windrush scandal, the hostile environment was relabelled the 'compliant environment'.

Irrespective of choice of name, the new environment has brought into sharp focus how immigration and nationality laws categorise people according to their date of entry, national origin, length of residence and attainments while in residence. These attributes confer legality if people come within relevant categories but exclude those who do not. It is easy to get these details wrong and even when the information are accurate, these categories reify and perpetuate various forms of inequality already faced by irregular migrants. Ethnic and racial minorities are often deemed or presumed to have irregular status and come under heightened scrutiny.

Law has been essential in this changing landscape of migration control. A series of Immigration Acts (2014 and 2016) excluded many irregular migrants from basic resources and services. These Acts introduced new requirements to check documents for establishing a right to work in the UK and even whether one can live in rented accommodation through deputisation of state functions to individuals. Charities and local governments have also been asked to report on

Privatisation of Migration Control: Power without Accountability?
Studies in Law, Politics, and Society, Volume 86B, 1–4

ISSN: 1059-4337/doi:10.1108/S1059-43372021000086B001

migration station with their budgets at risk of financial sanction in case of failure to comply with such requests. In the context of Brexit, such information has led to increased deportations of EU nationals who have been found sleeping rough or have some irregularities in their paperwork. Others such as asylum seekers have also found their lives becoming even more precarious as services are cut back or become sub-standard. The process of deputisation is a continuation of the crimmigration project. People who commit minor offences have suddenly become targeted with renewed vigour. Immigration control today is a replication of the military–industrial or prison–industrial complex where accountability of private actors is missing or minimal.

It is in this broad context that the chapters in the first section of this volume are on the private stakeholders in migration control. Private actors such as transport companies have been involved in immigration control since the early twentieth century, for instance in the United States through the Passenger Act 1902. In 1944, through the Convention on International Civil Aviation, nearly all (the now) EU countries increased carrier responsibility. The Asylum and Immigration Act 1999 warrants a regime of financial sanctions imposable against owners or agents of ships or aircrafts, who carry an individual who fails to produce a valid identification document, and where necessary, a visa. In Chapter 1, Aleksandra Wegera examines sanctions placed on carriers which lead to barriers to entry for asylum seekers. Wegera writes that carrier sanctions oblige commercial entities to check the validity of passengers' documents and deny boarding where no valid documents are shown, or where fraud is suspected. This law has meant that many male asylum seekers are deterred from safe journeys and lawful entry into the UK. Wegera places the spotlight on male migrants because she finds that most migrants who seek asylum are male: men accounted for 72% of asylum applications in 2017. But migration literature tends to overlook male migrants and their life experiences. Literature on male asylum seekers is often confined to their participation within the labour market, and little is written about the impact of migration journeys on men. Women and children are 'conceptualised of categories of vulnerability', and are seen as 'in need of additional support', so the focus is usually on their life situations.

In Chapter 2, Isabella Bertolini evaluates the role of medical professionals in implementing the hostile environment. She discusses the Memorandum of Understanding (MoU) between NHS Digital and the Home Office. Doctors and others in the medical profession organised to oppose the agreement and its effects. Challengers brought up issues of legality, effects on public health and wider economic implications as well as ethical issues. Yet the case study of the doctors and the memorandum also establishes how easily, and even without legislative authority, it was possible for the Home Office to gather data and deport people accessing health care.

In the next two chapters, Emily Rigler Gillingham and Harriet Parfitt write about employers and the responsibilities placed on them to report on employees and their immigration status. Gillingham writes that ethnocentrism is woven into the UK's approach to controlling irregular migration. Since January 1997, the UK has imposed sanctions on employers found to be employing irregular workers. Coercing employers into conducting immigration status checks makes it increasingly difficult for irregular migrants to secure employment opportunities, thus restricting their ability to sustain a tolerable life in the UK. The deputisation of employers, as well as other private entities, such as landlords, has become a pivotal element of what is commonly known as the 'hostile environment', an attempt to make UK life unbearable for irregular migrants. Gillingham finds that dehumanisation and exclusion are the two manifestations of ethnocentrism. Parfitt also focusses on employment but in the context of the agricultural industry and the Modern Slavery Act 2015. She finds that the vulnerabilities faced by irregular migrants are reinforced through the xenophobic narrative embodied within the law and the courts. The lack of priority afforded to modern slavery on the UK Policy Agenda has allowed a 'grey labour market' to develop. The government allows the commodification of workers within the supply chain to profit British businesses.

Overall, the chapters in the first section reveal that private parties perform a greater number of government like functions in the new environment and they do so with much less accountability. Privatisation reaches beyond individual participation in migration control in private capacity. To demonstrate how privatisation fundamentally alters the manner in which human capacity is viewed, the second section is on the political economy and commodification of migration. Innovations in capitalist modes of production have led to greater commodification of migration such as the role of the limited liability company in colonisation and the creation of investment routes to citizenship status. In Section II of this volume there are two chapters, one by Oppon and another by Kamber, which give further examples of the commodification of migration and migration measures.

Akosua-Rose Oppon traces from history how trade and the corporate structure have assisted imperialism in the case of the East India Company. The East India Company was a hybrid corporation. This merchant-state hybridity refers to the private function of the company as a joint-stock corporate established to trade and make profit for its shareholders, whilst simultaneously exercising public state governance as rulers of India. As the Company strived for profits, this was inherently contradictory to ruling a state of people. Its increasing public role alienated both Indians and the British government as it faced increasing criticism. Eventually state intervention increased until the Company operated as an agent for British imperialism, and its status continued to decline until the company was replaced by British rule. Oppon finds that the legacy of the East India Company represents the incompatibility of private actors taking on state responsibility.

Another example of commodification is found in the last chapter of this volume where Isobel Kamber looks at the British Tier 1 (Investor) visa. She asks if the Tier 1 visa has become a 'golden ticket' for obtaining residency and citizenship in the UK. The scheme offers an exclusive route to temporary residency in the UK in return for a £2 million investment in Britain. Kamber contends that the government has consistently underestimated the continual detrimental effects of offering such a scheme due to its economic advantages. Kamber claims that the scheme has imparted social disadvantage, highlighting the prevalence of inequality and the existence of a hierarchy of desired migrants and even increasing threats to public's safety. The problems with the scheme are 'lack of transparency;' 'inability to return any benefit to UK residents,' and for 'transforming the UK into a safe haven for money launderers'. Kamber does not stop at merely identifying these shortcomings, she argues that the overarching effect of offering such a visa is the marketisation of migration and commodification of secure migration status.

SECTION 1

PRIVATE STAKEHOLDERS IN MIGRATION CONTROL

CHAPTER 1

HOW ARE MIGRANTS, ESPECIALLY MALE ASYLUM SEEKERS, DETERRED FROM SAFE JOURNEYS AND LAWFUL ENTRY INTO THE UK THROUGH CARRIER SANCTIONS?

Aleksandra Wegera

ABSTRACT

Carrier sanctions oblige commercial entities to check the validity of passengers' documents and deny boarding where no valid documents are shown, or where fraud is suspected. The necessity to flee to safer countries at a time of particular political unrest has necessitated the use of fraudulent documents, which the sanction regime and subsequent case law have attempted to curtail. However, increased investigation into legitimacy of travel documents has induced the taking of dangerous routes to reach Britain. In particular, danger is posed by oncoming traffic, and where entry is attempted clandestinely, within lorries. Men, accounting for the majority of irregular entrants, are more likely to experience danger. Due to the very nature of their precarious position, potential asylum seekers may not hold travel documents, which induce the taking of dangerous routes to make asylum applications once in Britain. This chapter will attempts to link carrier sanctions, danger, and humanitarian obligations.

Keywords: Male migrants; carriers; sanctions; private actors; non-state agents; identification documents

Privatisation of Migration Control: Power without Accountability?
Studies in Law, Politics, and Society, Volume 86B, 7–22

Published under exclusive licence by Emerald Publishing Limited
ISSN: 1059-4337/doi:10.1108/S1059-43372021000086B002

1. INTRODUCTION

The control of immigration has been privatised through the involvement of non-state agents in managing of migration in, and out of, the UK. The role that has traditionally been performed exclusively by the state, and has demonstrated an element of sovereignty over a nation's borders, is now partially realised by private entities in lieu of public authorities (Menz, 2011). However, it is by no means an abdication of the state's sovereignty over the control of national borders, and carrier sanctions are better understood as an attempt to control migration flows, in particular of 'less desirable' groups, such as potential asylum seekers. This raises questions of the regime's legitimacy in light of international humanitarian obligations towards individuals fleeing persecution, many of whom are males. By discouraging undocumented or fraudulent entry through aeroplanes, the sanctions induce the making of life-threatening journeys through the English Channel. However, the link between the need to claim asylum, dangerous journeys, and carrier sanctions, has not yet been made in any English court, and the attempt to link the former two elements has been rejected by the Court of Appeal, due to the limited wording of legislation.

The Asylum and Immigration Act 1999 warrants a regime of financial sanctions imposable against owners or agents of ships or aircrafts, who carry an individual who fails to produce a valid identification document, and where necessary, a visa.[1] Sanctions inevitably induce carriers to participate in immigration control (Ruff, 1989) due to the threat of financial repercussions, which come as a direct result of carrying unauthorised passengers, and also indirectly, through the need to meet accommodation and deportation costs of passengers.

The first and second part of this chapter will explore the concept of masculinity within migration, and will suggest that male migrants are likely to take dangerous routes to reach their goal destination. The rationales for carrier sanctions will be scrutinised in the third part of this chapter, and it will be suggested that the regime seeks to indirectly limit the entry of 'undesirables', in particular asylum seekers. The fourth section will assess the impact of carrier sanctions imposed through Section 40 of the Immigration and Asylum Act 1999 on the actions of airline personnel. It will be suggested that the sanction regime induces an anxious and vigilant approach to the checking of passengers' documents and eligibility to travel, and that this task is carried out by non-specialist staff. Lastly, the compatibility of international obligations and the carrier sanction regime will be considered. Overall, it will be argued that strict immigration controls, strengthened by sanctions in Section 40, are likely to compel male migrants to engage in illegal and dangerous means of entry, in light of carriers' enforcement of entry requirements.

2. THE CONCEPT OF 'MASCULINITY' IN MIGRATION

Literature on male asylum seekers is often confined to their participation within the labour market (Chavez & Altman, 2017), and little is written about the impact of migration journeys on men. Instead, women and children are 'conceptualised of categories of vulnerability', and are seen as 'in need of additional support' (Baldwin-Edwards, Blitz, & Crawley, 2018). The lack of literature about the impact of males' journeys is not justified, since men accounted for 72% of asylum applications in 2017 (Home Office, 2018). Significantly, the statistics may not account for clandestine entrants whose presence in the UK is undetected, but who arguably took the most dangerous of routes of entry into Britain. For reasons that will be discussed later, male asylum seekers are amongst the groups most likely to be affected by the sanction regime.

Ideas of migrant masculinities in the West have generally been negative. Scheibelhofer (2012) suggests that securitisation of migration has 'reframed' the male migrant as a 'security threat', and has attributed to them a label of danger in particular towards the nation's women (Scheibelhofer, 2012). What followed is an imagery of 'sham asylum seekers' heading West, inter alia to be violent to or 'rape *our* women' (Scheibelhofer, 2012). Griffiths (2015) argues that these unjustified assumptions as to migrant masculinity affect the asylum application and welfare system, and migration policies that regulate entry. Indeed, Courtenay (2000) supports this, writing that they are based on an assumption that men have 'innate psychological needs for gender-stereotypic traits'. As such, men are 'encouraged to conform to stereotypic beliefs and behaviours' (Courtenay, 2000), such as that they are 'independent, self-reliant, strong, robust and tough' (Courtenay, 2000). As will be shown, carrier sanctions enforce entry requirements, leading to dangerous journeys being attempted into the UK.

Furthermore, Griffiths notes that migrants' immigration struggles are 'interlinked with their own senses of self as men', many of which result in men believing that they have not fulfilled their role as a male.[2] This pressure may arise from the idea of masculinity which operates *within* communities within which migrant men operate. As Kandel and Massey note, 'migration becomes a rite of passage, and those who do not attempt it are seen as lazy, unenterprising, and undesirable' as mates' (Massey et al., 1993). Therefore, it is possible that ideas of 'what it means to be an accepted man in society',[3] as well as restrictive immigration controls, lead men to forego safety in order to reach the UK. They may feel the need to demonstrate and fulfil their masculinity, which is in itself causes harm.

3. ILLEGAL ENTRY THROUGH DANGEROUS ROUTES

Migrants who seek to enter the UK may do so by travelling on an aeroplane, on the Eurostar train, or by coach or bus on a ferry or the Eurotunnel. Scholten notes that it may be dangerous for those seeking to flee a war-torn country to approach the authorities for documents (Scholten & Terlouw, 2014). Thus, due to financial constraints or lack of identification documents, migrants may engage in irregular means of entry. Furthermore, some migrants may wish to enter undetected by the immigration or asylum system, because this would allow them to work in an unregulated sector to support their livelihood (House of Commons Home Affairs Committee, 2015, p. 7).

The port of Calais is the 'closest entry point to the UK from Europe' (House of Commons Home Affairs Committee, 2015, p. 3). There has been wide media coverage of the presence of migrants in Calais, who use Calais as a 'staging post' before illegal entry into the UK (House of Commons Home Affairs Committee, 2015, p. 3). Despite the dismantling of migrant camps in 2016, and the wide availability of safe travel across the Channel, many vulnerable migrants may not use the established travel facilities to enter into the UK. Instead, as the Jack Straw White Paper for a 'firmer' immigration policy suggested in 1998, 'the introduction of carriers' liability legislation and greater vigilance by airline staff at ports of embarkation has seen a resurgence in clandestine traffic' (The Secretary of State for the Home Department, 1998). Thus, individuals may conceal themselves in vehicles to secure entry. Similarly to Calais in France, Immigration Inspectorate acknowledge that Dover 'stands apart' from other UK ports, because the 'threat of clandestine entry is understood to be higher at Dover' (David Bolt Independent Chief Inspector of Borders and Immigration, 2018, p. 6). This is because of the 'short transit time', 'low cost passenger fares', and 'high volume of RoRo traffic' (David Bolt Independent Chief Inspector of Borders and Immigration, 2018, p. 29), which are viewed opportunistically by individuals seeking to cross the Channel. In January 2019 two migrants were found concealed in mattresses, which were being carried on top of a vehicle (Bulman, 2019). Danger may also arise due to suffocation in the back of the lorry, as was the case for 71 individuals in 2014, 59 of whom were male (The Guardian, 2018). In recent years, attempts have been made to facilitate the discovery of clandestine entrants during customs checks, for example, by using carbon dioxide probes, detection dogs, and heartbeat monitors.[4] As an alternative to concealed entry, migrants may seek to travel the Channel by a small boat, often with the help of human smugglers (BBC, 2019). Undeniably, this exposes migrants to unpredictable and dangerous atmospheric conditions (Henley, 2018), the lack of lifejackets (Montgomery, 2018), and high volume of commercial sea traffic on the Channel. The dangers at sea are much more pronounced on the Mediterranean, but irregular journeys through the Channel expose migrants to being hit by oncoming traffic (Calais Migrant Solidarity), suffocation, or being crushed by palettes (Calais Migrant Solidarity). Many of such incidents are unreported (Calais Migrant Solidarity).

The case of *R* v. *Haroun*[5] demonstrates the dangerous routes embarked upon by migrants in pursuit of entry into the UK. Haroun fled Sudan by travelling through Egypt and Libya; he reached Folkestone by walking through the Channel Tunnel, thereby exposing himself to trains travelling up to 100 mph. This resulted in a charge of causing obstruction on the railway.[6] The facts are analogous to the latter case of *R* v. *Mirahessari*.[7] Although there is no prima facie direct causal link between carrier sanctions and this dangerous journey, because Haroun did not travel by aeroplane, the use of carrier sanctions has been seen by academics as a driving factor to migrants' use of dangerous means to reach their goal destination. Scholten writes that by definition, asylum seekers are unable to gain identification documents from their country of origin, so they may resort to the use of agents or clandestine entry.[8] This is because migrants may be unable to provide a passport and visa to the carrier at the point of embarkation, or their use of fraudulent documents may be detected. Indeed, due to the pressure on carriers to comply with their immigration control role, suspicion of fraud, or lack of documents, may result in rejection on boarding or subsequent deportation if detected by immigration officers in the destination country. Therefore, restrictive immigration policies may encourage, rather than halt, illegality, and the taking of greater risk (Rodenhauser, 2014).

However, responsibility for dangerous journeys into the UK cannot be entirely placed on the sanction regime. Instead, danger is directly caused by unscrupulous smugglers who fail to observe the safety of passengers, as was the case in the lorry tragedy.[9] Nonetheless, similarly to Scholten, Lax points to carrier sanctions which 'enforce the visa requirements', which are not achievable by asylum seekers, but which induce them to make dangerous journeys (Lax, 2008). On a similar basis, *Mirahessari* attempted to argue that *Haroun* was incorrectly decided, and that the defence under s31 Immigration and Asylum Act 1999 should have been accepted.[10] This defence excuses illegal acts if the individual can, inter alia, show a 'good cause for his illegal entry or presence'.[11] It is based on Article 31 of the Refugee Convention, which protects right to seek asylum.[12] Thus, *Mirahessari* attempted to demonstrate a causal link between political persecution and threat to life, and the obstruction he caused to the Channel Tunnel, which may be classed as a dangerous route into the UK. Although the Courts in *Haroun* and *Mirahessari* accepted that the men were genuine asylum seekers,[13] the Court of Appeal rejected the use of the s31 defence against the charges in both cases, because the defence only applied to the use of fraudulent documents to secure entry,[14] not to charges of obstruction on the railway. Therefore, it is clear that, where dangerous and illegal routes are taken by migrants, this will not absolve them from liability for obstruction to railway, but it may excuse the use of fraudulent documents for the purpose of entry.[15] Nonetheless, as it will be shown in Section 4, carriers may still be charged if they carry passengers with fraudulent documents, which makes it more difficult to successfully produce fraudulent documents to carriers.

4. JUSTIFYING CARRIERS' LIABILITY

There have been various attempts to justify the imposition of financial sanctions on carriers for carrying unauthorised or insufficiently documented passengers. Hollifield has written about the concept of the 'migration state', whereby control of immigration from the outside is 'as important as ensuring security and economic stability of the citizenry' (Hollifield, 1992). Andreouli and Howarth (2013) notes the prevalence of 'exclusionary undertones' in immigration policy generally. Similarly, Scholten identifies that the 'growing number of undocumented arrivals' in the second half of the 1990s has created a need to involve more actors in the control of immigration.[16] The Schengen Agreement of 1985 (Craig & De Burca, 2016), which introduced passport-free movement within participating European Economic Area member states, is perceived as a contributory instrument to the 'leniency' of border control.[17] Although the UK opted out of this agreement, the agreement abolished internal border points between participating member states. Thus, whilst documents are still checked upon entry into the UK, the requirement of visas has been abolished for travel in and out of Italy and Greece, which are first countries African asylum seekers will reach.[18] Therefore, together with increasing availability of cheaper flights, movement throughout the EU has been made less difficult (Cochrane, 2015). In response, Directive 2001/51/EC established that member states should 'introduce provisions laying down the obligations of carriers transporting foreign nationals', with the express aim of 'combating illegal immigration effectively'.[19] Therefore, the amended 1999 Act may be perceived as a product of the desire to prevent illegal movement.

In addition to the prevention of *illegal* migration, Rodenhauser writes that the introduction of carrier sanctions has allowed the state to 'add another brick in the wall designed to halt migration flows', by 'targeting asylum seekers'.[20] It does so by emphasising that carriers (thus expanding the role beyond immigration officers) check for genuine identification documents and visas. Due to their precarious situation, asylum seekers may find it even more difficult to produce valid identification documents, let alone visas.[21] Thus, Rumford notes that carrier sanctions allow the UK to pursue 'selective and targeted bordering' policies (Rumford, 2006), which would allow it to reduce the entry of 'undesirable migrants' (Rumford, 2006, p. 158). On the basis of the perception of the asylum seeker as an 'other', they are considered as a 'threat to the state and society within it' (Innes, 2010). Interestingly, he asserts that 'danger is inherent to that relationship', whereby it follows that alienating an 'outsider' may be justified by the desire to assert the nation's identity, and its security.

The 'othering' may also be due to the financial cost associated with asylum applications, provisions of welfare, and deportations of unsuccessful applicants. The government felt that many asylum applications were bogus, inter alia because the individuals travelled around the world in order to make the application at UK ports,[22] and it based its belief on the increased number of asylum applications at ports of entry (Shah P, *Refugees, race and the legal concept of asylum in Britain* (Shah, 2000, p. 146)). The idea of carrier sanctions as a filter to immigration is not unmeritorious, because an attempt to select migrants is evident from the Immigration Act 1971. This Act introduced visas for nationalities, some of which brought the most asylum claims at the time of introduction. Although the former Immigration (Carriers' Liability) Act 1987 does not make reference to asylum seekers, section 1(1)(b) required carriers to ensure that passengers hold visas, where required. This requirement is still in place in the amended 1999 Act. Therefore, Nicholson further emphasises the role of carriers in facilitating the selection of migrants, because the regime requires passengers to produce visas to their carrier before embarkation. The compatibility of carrier sanction legislation with international obligations in relation to asylum seekers will be considered later. At this stage, it is observed that there is support for the argument that carrier sanctions may be motivated on grounds of selection, and the desire to prevent some migrants from `accessing a state's [humanitarian] protection procedures'.[23]

The involvement of the carrier may be justified on practical grounds. The carrier is seen as capable of 'disrupting misconduct by withholding cooperation' from the wrongdoer (Kraakman, 1986, p. 53). Cooperation may be withheld by preventing the passenger from boarding, or preventing their clandestine entry into the UK if detected. Carriers, unlike immigration officers, are appropriately placed to detect illegality because they have physical access to the misconduct.[24] In the case of commercial carriers, this is before embarkation. Therefore, carriers are strategically placed, and may help to combat illegal immigration, as well as prevent some asylum seekers from entering the remit of the UK's protection. In practice, many entrants will enter clandestinely though dangerous routes.

5. CARRIERS' PENALTY SCHEME FOR IMPROPERLY UNDOCUMENTED PASSENGERS

5.1. Operation of the Scheme

Section 40 of the Immigration and Asylum Act 1999 governs the carrier penalty regime. It states that where a carrier transports an individual into the UK, but who 'fails to produce an immigration document'[25] or required visa[26] to an immigration officer, the owner of the ship or aircraft may be required to pay the sum of £2,000 per undocumented passenger.[27] Since 2002, the scheme ceased to apply to coach, bus, or train carriers,[28] although carriers using these modes of transport are now liable to sanctions for clandestine entrants.[29] Therefore, penalties apply to any passenger who is neither a British citizen nor a commonwealth citizen.[30] In 2017, there were 135.2 million instances of entry into the UK, which demonstrates the size of the responsibility which is placed upon carriers (Home Office, 2018). Border Agency identified 4,000 cases of insufficiently documented arrivals in 2012 (Grant Oliver at Home Office, 2012).

5.2. Identity Documents and Visa Checks

The effect of Section 40 is that carriers, mostly through airline personnel, must ask passengers to provide passports or European Economic Area identity cards. They must decide whether such documents are genuine, and whether they belong to the passenger. Ruff identifies that one of the motivations for this provision was to discourage the use of false documents, which amongst other purposes, the Government felt were being used to make 'bogus' asylum claims.[31] Although carriers are strategically placed in the immigration control regime, because they have direct contact with passengers, the involvement of airline personnel may be objected to for the lack of personnel's immigration training.[32] Airline personnel receive some basic compulsory training on the authenticity of immigration documents. However, it is unlikely that airline staff will be able to always correctly determine authenticity without the use of specialist equipment, given the 'significant increase in the number and sophistication of forgeries' (Nicholson, 1997). This may lead to a failure to fulfil their statutory duty.[33] Alternatively, it may lead to an overcautious checking of documents, or strategic rejections of documents from certain countries.

5.3. 'Reasonably Apparent' Forgery

In response to this concern, the previous 1987 Act, as well as the current regime in the 1999 Act, indemnifies carriers from liability where the falsity of the document was not 'reasonably apparent'.[34] Although the Act does not expand on the meaning of 'reasonably apparent' forgery, uncertainty as to the meaning of 'reasonable appearance' of forgery was raised in *Ryanair* v. *SSHD*.[35] The case concerned question as to meaning of 'reasonably apparent' forgery, in a case of imposition of penalty against Ryanair for carrying two individuals who presented false Greek passports. The judges imported 'basic concepts justice and the rule of law',[36] into to the standards required of carriers. The facts of the case demonstrate the relative difficulty which carriers are faced with, because the forgery was not detected by the carrier, nor the Spanish border police, but was found by UK border officers. There was no colour shift on word 'Hellas' when tilted,[37] and the court found that there was 'rather obvious signs of tampering with the document'. The court clarified that personnel would be required to have only a 'basic level of knowledge on identifying false documents', and would not be required to undertake 'highly detailed examination'.[38] This standard may be reached without the use of specialist equipment.[39] The new threshold also requires it to be reasonable to expect personnel to know where to look for irregularities. Therefore, it found that the forgery was not reasonably apparent. Despite the tampering in this case, the court was persuaded by the 'very inconsistent approach and inconsistent standards being applied' by the Secretary of State.[40]

Interestingly, the Government has recently encouraged the use of identification document validation technology. In its guidance, it required airports to reach the highest level of assurance as to documents' validity, which requires them to conduct 'many checks in identify document security features'.[41] In contrast, a manual check is considered to provide the lowest level of assurance. Although the level of assurance required of carriers is not identified, and this guidance is only persuasive because it refers to airports generally, it acknowledges the fact that many airlines will only conduct manual checks of documents. Whilst such technology may allow more certainty as to the validity of the documents, case law and immigration guidance do not require carriers to use specialist equipment. Therefore, its lack of use is not surprising, given the lack of legal incentive to expend on specialist equipment.

5.4. Denial of Boarding

On the one hand, *Ryanair (2016)* demonstrates a lowering of the standard of investigation into authenticity of documents, which may suggest that carriers need not deny boarding in the case of doubt as to a document's validity. Indeed, payment of the penalty is demanded in only half of cases, inter alia due to the 'reasonable appearance' of fraud (Harper, 2013, p. 5). Yet, the impact of *Ryanair (2016)* is limited to cases of forged documents.

In contrast, the recent judgment in *Ryanair* v. *SSHD* (2018)[42] demonstrates the detail to which carriers must have regard when deciding whether to admit passengers. The case concerned an unsuccessful appeal against a penalty imposed on Ryanair for permitting a non-EEA passenger to board without a valid visa. Ryanair argued that the passenger carried a valid 'residence card', which entitled him to exercise free movement rights as a family-member of an EEA citizen. However, L. J. Newey stated that in order to satisfy the requirement of Article 10, the document needed to bear the words 'Residence card of a family member of a Union citizen',[43] as opposed to merely 'Family Member – Permanent Residence'. This difference may have been insignificant to carrier personnel. Reference to the Community within the document is seen as evidence of the entitlement to exercise of free movement rights. However, this judgment does not facilitate the entry of undocumented asylum seekers, because it is unlikely that asylum seekers will have a right to free movement. The vast majority of asylum applications in the UK are made by nationals of non-EEA countries (Blinder, 2019), which places them outside of the scope of free movement rights for EU citizens and possibly their dependent families. Furthermore, it is unlikely that asylum seekers will have other documents which may help to demonstrate entitlement to free movement by 'other means'.[44] The court acknowledged that tourists are unlikely to carry all such documents,[45] and it is reasonable that the asylum seeker's country of origin is even more unlikely to provide documents due to political unrest. Therefore, whilst *Ryanair* (2016) may be an evidence of the clarification and decreasing pressure put upon carriers in relation to forged documents, *Ryanair* (2018) has little impact on the undocumented migrant, save for allowing a symbolic opportunity to prove free movement entitlement in other ways than through immigration documents.

A discussion of dangerous routes embarked upon by migrants has been made in Section 2 of this chapter, and it was suggested that Section 40 may be seen as a deterrent to entry into the UK by safer modes of transport, particularly where individuals do not possess the requisite immigration documents. In Section 1 it was suggested that this may have heightened effect on males. In relation to asylum seekers, the lack of these documents may arise due to rushed exit from a country, or if it is too dangerous to approach the country's authorities for documents.[46] This may induce passengers to use fraudulent documents, and the carrier is likely to perceive the undocumented passenger as an 'economic threat'.[47] For example, asylum seekers may be denied boarding by the carrier on ground of suspicion that the document is fraudulent, notwithstanding the potential for the undocumented individual to subsequently make a meritorious asylum application once in the UK, which could remove the fine. Scholten explains this problem by reference to Haas' work on carriers' membership of an epistemic community. Although Haas' work argues that the carrier could be part of an 'epistemic community', whereby carriers belong to a group of experts in travel documents and entry requirements, Scholten denies that carriers may ever belong.[48] This can be explained by the curtailment in the 'autonomy to make norms'.[49] Whilst carriers make their own norms as to transport conditions and terms of business, they are merely 'semi-autonomous when implementing government rules on immigration control'.[50] On a practical level, the 'internal norm' of the carrier is to transport high quantities of passengers in the 'most cost-efficient manner'.[51] In contrast, the desire to limit migration flows and to exercise sovereignty over borders is not an element in which the carrier wishes to participate. Instead, their interest 'will always be commercial'.[52]

The charge was increased from £1,000 to £2,000 in 1999.[53] However, the Harper consultation suggests that the penalty should be increased to £3,500, in order to bring the penalty amount 'in line with inflation'.[54] The consultation suggested that the optimum penalty is £7,000, in order to increase the deterrence effect of the sanctions, with the effect of 'reducing the number of [undocumented individuals] coming to the UK'. This justification is dubious, since Ryanair alone was fined £400,000 in 2015.[55] In addition, the number of insufficiently documented migrants depends not entirely on the stringency of carrier sanctions but on external factors such as state of politics abroad and domestic asylum policy. Finally, whilst acknowledging that only half of cases demand payment of cases,[56] the consultation fails to acknowledge that the continuing operation of the s40 defence will continue to exempt many carriers from penalty, thus arguably reducing its deterrent effect. From the findings in this and previous sections, it can be concluded that a higher penalties risk more vigorous checking, which would induce even more irregular journeys due to the inability to rely on fraudulent documents.

6. CARRIER SANCTION REGIME AS A MECHANISM OF DEPARTING FROM INTERNATIONAL HUMANITARIAN OBLIGATIONS

A major humanitarian obligation in respect of asylum seekers to-be (and thus many passengers who may be denied boarding by carriers) is the duty to provide a right to 'seek and enjoy asylum' if a person has a 'well-founded fear of being persecuted' on the basis of some protected characteristic.[57] The 1951 Refugee Convention provides protection through acknowledgement of 'refugee' status (Convention Relating to the Status of Refugees ('1951 Refugee Convention'), Article 1).[58] Furthermore, Article 14 UDHR provides that 'everyone has a right to seek and enjoy in other countries asylum from protection'.[59] It follows that *states* are internationally obliged to 'provide access to their asylum procedures' (Bell & Hirsch, 2017), to allow individuals to *seek* asylum. This obligation does not necessarily create a correlative duty on states to accept asylum claims. Nonetheless, 'access to asylum depends practically on access to a place of refuge' (Costello, 2012) because the individual must reach the state's territory to apply. Thus, it is arguable that carrier sanctions, through enforcing 'unachievable' document and visa requirements against asylum seekers, *de facto* deny regular access to the country where refuge could be sought. Rodenhauser notes that this is because carriers *de facto* perform immigration selection on ground of documents, and not the individual's circumstances, such as persecution.[60] Thus, Hirsch and Bell criticised states for using domestic laws to 'ignore' international obligations.[61] Therefore, access to 'humanitarian protection *de facto* depends on the ability to enter clandestinely'.[62] Male migrants are the most likely to take dangerous journeys, due to inter alia internalised gender-specific traits, and external (societal) pressure to prove masculinity, for example, through seeking safety or economic relief by migration.

However, despite criticism, carrier sanctions have not recognised as being contrary to international law. This may be because whilst the right to leave one's country is internationally recognised, there is no right to enter any country unconditionally,[63] and states are at liberty to impose entry requirements.

6.1. Obligations on Whom?

Although as a general rule states are liable for actions of non-state actors only in certain circumstances, there is support for the contention that conduct of carriers is 'attributable to the state' when 'acting in accordance with carrier sanction legislation'.[64] Since the legislation confers part of the state's authority' to carriers,[65] the former will be responsible for 'internationally wrongful acts committed by the carrier when fulfilling their responsibilities under legislation'.[66] Thus, there is scope to argue that privatisation has not absolved states from humanitarian responsibility in principle.

6.2. Duty of Non-refoulement

States are bound by the duty of non-refoulment in Article 33 of the Refugee Convention, which imposes a duty on states to not return asylum seekers to countries where they could suffer persecution. It could be argued that carriers' denial of boarding of asylum seekers to-be is contrary to the duty of non-refoulement.

However, outsourcing performance to carriers, who often operate extraterritorially, allows states to avoid some humanitarian obligations, because the carriers act outside of the jurisdiction of the state which owes particular humanitarian obligations. This was made clear by the House of Lords in *Prague Airport*[67] case, where the duty was construed territorially.[68] Therefore, it is limited to individuals who have already left their country of persecution. Since carriers' duties under carrier sanction legislation exist at the time of boarding, the duty of non-refoulement do not extend to extra-territorial activities.

It follows that the privatisation of immigration control has allowed the UK to avoid, as opposed to dismiss, its international humanitarian obligations. These obligations continue to exist, but the simultaneous outsourcing and offshoring[69] of immigration control allows the UK to create a barrier to responsibility in relation to receiving asylum claims, and potential non-refoulement issues at rejection of boarding.

7. CONCLUSION

The carrier sanction regime can be described as an 'outwards shift in decision making away from the state',[70] towards private actors. However, it does not constitute a removal of the state's responsibility for asylum seekers per se. Instead, it knowledgeably dodges liability for non-refoulement, by inducing the carrier to deny entry extraterritorially, thus preventing Article 33[71] from biting. L. J. Newey said in *obiter* that there is nothing wrong with discouraging undocumented travel,[72] but there is overwhelming academic support in particular from Rodenhauser, Lax, and Scholten, to the contrary, in particular in relation to asylum seekers. Rather curiously, the regime that expressly sought to reduce undocumented entry via air travel has *induced* undocumented clandestine entry, in absence of any other means to reach the country in order to make asylum applications. The dangerous routes embarked upon by migrants in pursuit of the UK are clear from migrant accounts, studies, and case law before English courts.[73] Thus, it appears that the regime, perhaps unknowingly, amplifies males' internalised gender-specific traits, and external (societal) pressure to prove masculinity through migration. This only adds to the danger experienced by asylum seekers to-be.

NOTES

1. Immigration and Asylum Act 1999, s1(a)–(b).
2. Griffiths [n10] 470.
3. Chavez and Altman [n4] 539.
4. David Bolt [n22] 29.
5. *R* v. *Haroun (Abdul Rahman)* unreported.
6. *R* v. *Mirahessari* [2016] EWCA Crim 1733, 2.
7. *R* v. *Mirahessari* [2016] EWCA Crim 1733, 2.
8. Scholten and Terlouw [n17] 306.
9. The Guardian. [n25].
10. *Mirahessari* [n34] 7.
11. Immigration and Asylum Act 1999, s31(1)(b).
12. Convention relating to the Status of Refugees, Article 31.
13. *Mirahessari* [n34]. 26.
14. *Mirahessari* [n34]. 23.
15. *Mirahessari* [n34]. 23.
16. Scholten and Terlouw [n17]. 297.
17. Scholten and Terlouw [n17]. 297.
18. House of Commons Home Affairs Committee [n18]. 10.
19. Directive 2001/51/EC, Paragraph 1.
20. Rodenhauser [n37]. 224.
21. Lax [n39]. 322.
22. Ruff [n3]. 484.
23. Rodenhauser [n37]. 224.
24. Scholten and Terlouw [n17]. 292.
25. Immigration and Asylum Act 1999 s40(1)(a).
26. Immigration and Asylum Act 1999 s40(1)(b).
27. Immigration and Asylum Act 1999 s40(2).
28. Nationality, Immigration and Asylum Act 2002, Schedule 8, Para. 12.
29. Nationality, Immigration and Asylum Act 2002, Schedule 8, Para 2.
30. Immigration Act 1971, s2(1)(a)–(b).
31. Ruff [n3]. 484.
32. Rodenhauser [n37]. 229.
33. Immigration and Asylum Act 1999, s40(1)(a)–(b).
34. Immigration and Asylum Act 1999 s40(5)(a).
35. *Ryanair* v. *Secretary of State for the Home Department* [2016] 1 WLUK 356.
36. *Ryanair* v. *Secretary of State for the Home Department* [2016] 1 WLUK 356, 92.
37. *Ryanair* v. *Secretary of State for the Home Department* [2016] 1 WLUK 356, 6.
38. *Ryanair* v. *Secretary of State for the Home Department* [2016] 1 WLUK 356, 89.
39. *Ryanair* v. *Secretary of State for the Home Department* [2016] 1 WLUK 356, 24.
40. *Ryanair* v. *Secretary of State for the Home Department* [2016] 1 WLUK 356, 84.

41. Home Office, Immigration Guidance: Identification Document Validation Technology (2018), 2.2.
42. *Ryanair* v. *Secretary of State for the Home Department [2018] EWCA Civ 899.*
43. *Ryanair* v. *Secretary of State for the Home Department [2018] EWCA Civ 899,* 35.
44. *Ryanair* v. *Secretary of State for the Home Department* [n85]. 43.
45. *Ryanair* v. *Secretary of State for the Home Department* [n85]. 43.
46. Scholten and Terluow [n17]. 306.
47. Scholten and Terluow [n17]. 291
48. Scholten and Terluow [n17]. 311
49. Scholten and Terluow [n17]. 296
50. Scholten and Terluow [n17]. 288
51. Scholten and Terluow [n17]. 291
52. Scholten and Terluow [n17]. 288.
53. Immigration and Asylum Act 1999 s40(2).
54. Harper MP [n84]. 5.
55. *Ryanair* v. *Secretary of State for the Home Department* [n77]. 28.
56. Harper MP [n84]. 5.
57. Convention Relating to the Status of Refugees ('1951 Refugee Convention'), Article 1.
58. Convention Relating to the Status of Refugees ('1951 Refugee Convention'), Article 1.
59. Universal Declaration of Human Rights, Art 14(1).
60. Rodenhauser [n37]. 228.
61. Bell and Hirsch [n104]. 430.
62. Bell and Hirsch [n104]. 424.
63. Bell and Hirsch [n104].
64. Rodenhauser [n37]. 223.
65. Rodenhauser [n37]. 232.
66. Rodenhauser [n37]. 232.
67. *R (On the application of European Roma Rights Centre)* v. *Immigration Officer, Prague Airport [2004] UKHL 55.*
68. *R (On the application of European Roma Rights Centre)* v. *Immigration Officer, Prague Airport [2004] UKHL* 53
69. Rodenhauser [n37]. 246.
70. Rodenhauser [n37]. 234.
71. Convention Relating to the Status of Refugees ('1951 Refugee Convention'), Article 33.
72. *Ryanair* v. *Secretary of State for the Home Department* [85]. 53.
73. *Mirahessari* [n34].

BIBLIOGRAPHY

Andreouli, E., & Howarth, C. (2013). National identity, citizenship, and immigration: Putting identity in context. *Journal for the Theory of Social Behaviour*, *43*(3), 361–382.

Baldwin-Edwards, M., Blitz, B., & Crawley, H. (2018). The politics of evidence-based policy in Europe's 'migration crisis'. *Journal of Ethnics and Migration Studies*, *45*(12), 2139–2155. doi:10.1080/1369183X.2018.1468307

BBC. (2019, February 18). Channel migrant boat off Dover held 34 people. Retrieved from https://www.bbc.co.uk/news/uk-england-kent-47282916. Accessed on February 23, 2019.

Bell, N., & Hirsch, A. L. (2017). The right to have rights as a right to enter addressing a lacuna in the International Refugee Protection Regime. *Human Rights Review*, *18*, 417. doi:10.1007/s12142-017-0472-4

Blinder, S. (2019, January 4). Migration to the UK: Asylum and refugees. *Migration Observatory Oxford.* Retrieved from https://migrationobservatory.ox.ac.uk/resources/briefings/migration-to-the-uk-asylum/. Accessed on January 6, 2019.

Bloch, A., Sigona, N., & Zetter, R. (2011). Migration routes and strategies of young undocumented migrants in England: A qualitative perspective. *Ethnic and Racial Studies*, *34*(8), 1286–1302. doi:10.1080/01419870.2011.560276

Bloom, T., & Risse, V. (2014). Examining hidden coercion at state borders: Why carrier sanctions cannot be justified. *Ethics & Global Politics*, *7*(2). doi:10.3402/egp.v7.24736

Bouhenia, M., Farhat, J. B., Coldiron, M. E., Abdallah, S., Visentin, D., Neuman, M., … Cohuet, S. (2017). Quantitative survey on health and violence endured by refugees during their journey and in Calais, France. *International Health*, *9*(6), 335–342. doi:10.1093/inthealth/ihx040

Brian, T., & Laczko, F. (2014). *Fatal journeys: Tracking lives lost during migration*. Geneva: International Organization for Migration.

Bulman, M. (2019, January 1). Two men discovered hidden inside mattresses crossing from Morocco to Spain. Retrieved from https://www.independent.co.uk/news/world/europe/migrants-mattresses-spain-europe-people-smuggling-refugees-asylum-jon-inarritu-a8706396.html. Accessed on January 2, 2019.

Calais Migrant Solidarity. Deaths at the Calais border. Retrieved from https://calaismigrantsolidarity.wordpress.com/deaths-at-the-calais-border/. Accessed on March 11, 2019.

Chavez, S., & Altman, C. (2017). Gambling with life: Masculinity, risk, and danger in the lives of unauthorized migrant roofers. *American Journal of Industrial Medicine*, *60*, 537. doi:10.1002/ajim.22721

Cherubini, F. (2015). *Asylum Law in the European Union*. Oxon: Routledge.

Clayton, G. (2016). *Textbook on immigration and Asylum Law* (7th ed.). Oxford: Oxford University Press.

Cochrane, F. (2015). *Migration and security in the global age: Diaspora communities and conflict*. New York, NY: Routledge.

Connell, R. W., & Messerschmidt, J. W. (2005). Hegemonic masculinity: Rethinking the concept. *Gender and Society*, *19*(6). doi:10.1177/0891243205278639

Costello, C. (2012). Courting access to asylum in Europe: Recent supranational jurisprudence explored. *Human Rights Law Review*, *12*, 287–339. doi:10.1093/hrlr/ngs011

Courtenay, W. H. (2000). Constructions of masculinity and their influence on men's well-being: A theory of gender and health. *Social Science and Medicine*, *5*, 1385–1401.

Craig, P., & De Burca, G. (2016). *EU Law: Text, cases, and materials* (6th ed.). Oxford: Oxford University Press.

David Bolt Independent Chief Inspector of Borders and Immigration. (2018). *An inspection of Border Force operations at south coast seaports*. London: Independent Chief Inspector of Borders and Immigration.

Gamlen, A. (2015). 'An inborn restlessness': Migration and exile in a turbulent world. *Migration Studies*, *3*(3), 307–314. doi:10.1093/migration/mnv020

Gammeltoft-Hansen, T. (2012, April 12). Can privatization kill? Retrieved from https://www.nytimes.com/2012/04/02/opinion/when-it-comes-to-immigration-privatization-can-kill.html. Accessed on October 5, 2018.

Grant Oliver at Home Office. (2012, October 15). Carriers' liability penalty charge consultation. Retrieved from https://assets.publishing.service.gov.uk/government/uploads/system/uploads/attachment_data/file/147875/consultation-impact-assessment.pdf. Accessed on February 10, 2019.

Grey, C. (2015). *Justice and authority in Immigration Law*. Oxford: Hart Publishing.

Griffiths, M. (2015). "Here, man is nothing!": Gender and policy in an asylum context. *Men and Masculinities*, *18*(4), 468–488. doi:10.1177/1097184X15575111

Harper, M. P. M. (2013). *Carriers' liability charge: Consultation on proposals to increase the level of charge and introduce a new incentives scheme*. London: Home Office.

Henley, J. (2018, December 31). "This is the only way now": Desperate Iranians attempt Channel crossing. Retrieved from https://www.theguardian.com/uk-news/2018/dec/31/this-is-the-only-way-now-desperate-iranians-attempt-channel-crossing. Accessed on January 2, 2019.

Hollifield, J. (1992). Migration and international relations: Cooperation and control in the European Community. *International Migration Review*, *26*(2), 568–595.

Home Office. (2016, February 22). *Immigration statistics, October to December 2017: Data tables* (2nd ed.). Retrieved from https://www.gov.uk/government/statistics/immigration-statistics-october-to-december-2017-data-tables. Accessed on February 10, 2019.

Home Office. (2018, August 23). National statistics: How many people do we grant asylum or protection to? Retrieved from https://www.gov.uk/government/publications/immigration-statistics-year-ending-june-2018/how-many-people-do-we-grant-asylum-or-protection-to. Accessed on December 18, 2018.

Innes, A. (2010). When the threatened become the threat: The construction of asylum seekers in British Media Narratives. *International Relations Journal*, *24*(4), 456–477. doi:10.1177/0047117810385882

Kraakman, R. (1986). Gatekeepers: The anatomy of a third-party enforcement strategy. *Journal of Law, Economics and Organization*, *2*(1), 53–104.

Kritzman-Amir, T. (2011). Privatization and delegation of State Authority in asylum systems. *Law & Ethics Human Rights*, *5*(1), 194–215. doi:10.2202/1938-2545.1057

Lahav, G. (1998). Immigration and the state: The devolution and privatisation of immigration control in the EU. *Journal of Ethnic and Migration Studies*, *24*(4), 675–694. doi:10.1080/1369183X.1998.9976660

Lax, V. M. (2008). Must EU borders have doors for refugees? On the compatibility of Schengen Visas and carriers' sanctions with EU Member States' obligations to provide international protection to refugees. *European Journal of Migration and Law*, *10*, 315–364. doi:10.1163/157181608X338180

Lethbridge, J. (2017). *Privatisation of migration & refugee services & other forms of state disengagement*. London: University of Greenwich.

Massey, D. S., Arango, J., Hugo, G., Kouaouci, A., Pellegrino, A., & Taylor, E. (1993). Theories of international migration: A review and appraisal. *Population and Development Review*, *19*(3), 431–466.

McNamara, F. (2017). *Externalised and privatised procedures of EU migration control and border control: A study of EU Member State control and legal responsibility European University Institute*. Florence: European University Institute.

Menz, G. (2011). Neo-liberalizm, privatization and the outsourcing of migration management: A five-country comparison. *Competition and Change*, *15*(2), 116–135. doi:10.1179/102452911X13025292603633

Montgomery, K. (2018). A hard life for refugee families. In M. M. Eboch (Eds.), *Migrants and refugees* (pp. 30–36). London: Greenhaven Publishing.

Nicholson, F. (1997). Implementation of the Immigration (Carriers' Liability) Act 1987: Privatising immigration functions at the expense of international obligations. *International & Comparative Law Quarterly*, *46*(3), 586–634.

Peers, S., Guild, E., Acosta Arcarazo, D., Groenendijk, K., & Moreno-Lax, V. (2012). *EU Immigration and Asylum Law (Text and Commentary: Second Revised Edition: Volume 2: EU Immigration Law* (2nd ed.). Leiden: Martinus Nijhoff Publishers.

Prabhat, D. (2018). *Britishness, belonging and citizenship: Experiencing Nationality Law*. Bristol: Policy Press University of Bristol.

Rodenhauser, T. (2014). Another brick in the wall: Carrier sanctions and the privatization of immigration control. *International Journal of Refugee Law*, *26*, 223–247. doi:10.1093/ijrl/eeu020

Ruff, A. (1989). The Immigration (Carriers' Liability) Act 1987: Its implications for refugees and airlines. *International Journal of Refugee Law*, *1*(4), 481–500.

Rumford, C. (2006). Theorizing borders. *European Journal of Social Theory*, *9*(2), 155–169. doi:10.1177/1368431006063330

Scheibelhofer, P. (2012). From health check to muslim test: The shifting politics of governing migrant masculinity. *Journal of International Students*, *33*, 319–332. doi:10.1080/07256868.2012.673474

Scholten, S. (2015). *The privatisation of immigration control through carrier sanctions: The role of private transport companies in Dutch and British immigration control*. Leiden: Martinus Nijhoff.

Scholten, S., & Minderhoud, P. (2008). Regulating immigration control: Carrier sanctions in the Netherlands. *European Journal of Migration and Law*, *19*, 123–147. doi:10.1163/157181608X317309

Scholten, S., & Terlouw, A. (2014). Private carriers as experts in immigration control. In M. Ambrus et al. (Eds.), *The role of 'experts' in International and European decision-making processes: Advisors, decision makers or irrelevant actors* (pp. 288–312)? Cambridge: Cambridge University Press.

Shah, P. (2000). *Refugees, race and the legal concept of asylum in Britain*. London: Cavendish.

Stevens, D. (2004). *UK Asylum Law and Policy: Historical and contemporary perspectives*. London: Thompson.

The Guardian. (2018, June 14). Four men jailed over deaths of 71 migrants locked in lorry. Retrieved from https://www.theguardian.com/world/2018/jun/14/people-smuggling-gang-jailed-over-hungary-migrant-lorry-deaths. Accessed on November 14, 2018.

Wray, H. (2009). Moulding the migrant family. *Legal Studies*, *29*, 592–618. doi:10.1111/j.1748-121X.2009.00132

Zago, M. Z. (2018). Externalisation of border controls through carrier sanctions: Effects on refugees' rights and Member States' responsibility. Retrieved from http://arno.uvt.nl/show.cgi?fid=145761. Accessed on January 6, 2019.

GOVERNMENT PUBLICATIONS

Home Office, Immigration Guidance: Guidance on examining identity documents (2014).

Home Office, Immigration Guidance: Identification Document Validation Technology (2018), 2.2.

House of Commons Home Affairs Committee: The work of the Immigration Directorates (HC 902 Eighteenth Report of Session 2014-15, 2015).

The Secretary of State for the Home Department, Fairer, Faster and Firmer – A Modern Approach to Immigration Asylum (Cm 4018 1998)

United Nations. (1994). Report of the United Nations High Commissioner for Refugees. General Assembly Official Records, 49th Session.

UK CASE LAW

R (On the application of European Roma Rights Centre) v. *Immigration Officer, Prague Airport* [2004] UKHL 55.

R v. *Mirahessari* [2016] EWCA Crim 1733.

R v. *Haroun* (Abdul Rahman) unreported.

Ryanair v. *Secretary of State for the Home Department* [2016] 1 WLUK 356

Ryanair v. Secretary of State for the Home Department [2018] EWCA Civ 899.

UK LEGISLATION

Aliens Act 1905.

Convention Relating to the Status of Refugees ('1951 Refugee Convention').

Directive 2001/51/EC.

Immigration Act 1971.

Immigration (Carriers' Liability) Act 1987.

Immigration and Asylum Act 1999.

International Legislation and Treaties.

Nationality, Immigration and Asylum Act 2002.

Universal Declaration of Human Rights.

CHAPTER 2

BY WHAT MEANS ARE MEDICAL PROFESSIONALS ABLE TO REJECT HOSTILE ENVIRONMENT POLICY WITHIN THE NHS?

Isabella Bertolini

ABSTRACT

A Memorandum of Understanding (MoU) was uncovered in January 2017 detailing the sharing of patient data from NHS Digital to the Home Office. It signified a deepening of the hostile environment's presence in the NHS, and was comprehensively rejected by medical professionals. In November 2018, following extensive action calling for its removal, the MoU was withdrawn. This chapter explores how three factors: the lack of legal basis, wide reaching effects, and ethical conflicts of the MoU led to the success of this action, and aims to apply these lessons to other areas of hostile environment policy. It will be established that ethics proved the most influential factor in inciting the opposition, however, all factors may have been integral to the overall success. It shall be demonstrated that, although the success of this action promises much with regards to charging policy, it may be of limited applicability to other areas of the hostile environment.

Keywords: Hostile environment; medical; doctors; patients; deportation; data sharing

Privatisation of Migration Control: Power without Accountability?
Studies in Law, Politics, and Society, Volume 86B, 23–39

ISSN: 1059-4337/doi:10.1108/S1059-43372021000086B003

1. INTRODUCTION

In early 2017, the hostile environment deepened its grip on the NHS through a Memorandum of Understanding (MoU) (*Memorandum of Understanding Between Health and Social Care Information Centre and The Home Office and The Department Of Health*, January 2017) requiring the transfer of patient information from the NHS to the Home Office for the purposes of immigration enforcement. The agreement was withdrawn as a result of considerable opposition which centred around three core concerns; each of these will be examined in turn with the aims of revealing how they facilitated, legitimised and motivated the collective action taken. First, the lack of legal basis (Health and Social Care Committee, 2018b) will be explored as a facilitating factor in the MoU's withdrawal. Second, the effects on health seeking behaviour, risks to public health (Health and Social Care Committee, 2018b) and wider economic implications will illustrate why such action was deemed necessary. Third, the ethical objections to disclosure (Health and Social Care Committee, 2018b) will be established as the major contributing factor which unified and legitimised the opposition. This chapter aims to establish how each of these factors contributed to the successful dismantling of the MoU, and additionally, how these lessons may be extracted to strengthen opposition to other areas of hostile environment policy.

2. BACKGROUND

The hostile environment (or 'compliant environment') (Grierson, 2018) is a form of state exclusion (Bradley, 2018) which outsources responsibility for determining a person's residence status to private individuals, requiring them to restrict access to goods and services for anyone residing in the UK without leave (Bolt, 2019). It aims to create a cumulative deterrent effect on irregular immigration (Equality and Human Rights Commission, 2018) by intentionally constructing unappealing living conditions (Shahvisi, 2018). This 'sprawling web of immigration control' (Bradley, 2018, p. 10) involving banking, policing, employment, education, private renting and many other services, is particularly concerning with regard to its presence in healthcare. Weaponisation (Bhagawati, 2019) of the NHS under the hostile environment is twofold, comprising of data sharing and charging. Whilst the primary focus of this chapter is data sharing, we will come to see that the two policies are virtually indistinguishable in terms of their operation, impact and reception by the medical profession. As such, an account of the hostile environment in the NHS focussing exclusively on data sharing would be incomplete.

Charging policy requires those not 'ordinarily resident' (*National Health Service Act 2006*, s175; *Immigration Act 2014*, s39) to pay upfront (*National Health Service (Charges to Overseas Visitors) (Amendment) Regulations 2017*, Regulation 3(1A)) for non-emergent services at a rate of 150% (Department of Health and Social Care, 2019) of the cost of the service, or face being denied access to the treatment. This requires NHS staff to carry out ID-checks in order to determine who is chargeable (Department of Health and Social Care, 2019). Although the MoU has been withdrawn, data sharing still occurs *de facto* (Williams, 2018) as the NHS is obliged to share non-clinical data of patients with a debt of £500 or more with the Home Office (Bolt, 2019; Bulman, 2019; Department of Health and Social Care, 2019). The two policies are intrinsically linked, and it is therefore imperative to establish precisely why action against the MoU was so successful, and apply any such lessons to the 'Patients not Passports' (Potter, 2018) movement against the charging regime.

The MoU, uncovered by a freedom of information request in January 2017 (Silberner, 2018), enabled NHS Digital to share non-clinical patient data, such as addresses, with the Home Office in the interests of 'maintaining effective immigration controls' (MoU, 2017, para. 7.9). Just as data sharing continues in its absence, it also took place before its creation (Partridge, 2014). The MoU was merely intended to simplify this process. The agreement was implemented without public consultation (Hiam, Steele, & McKee, 2018) and without the consent or knowledge of the medical profession (Johnson, 2018). Unsurprisingly, opposition quickly ensued involving: 70,000 doctors, Doctors of the World, Liberty, Public Health England (PHE), the Royal College of Physicians and many others – all calling for the MoU's immediate suspension or withdrawal (Kmietowicz, 2018, p. 1; Silberner, 2018). The action taken included the creation of the 'Docs not Cops' group, 'Stop Sharing' and 'Care Don't Share' campaigns, open letters, reports, hearings and petitions, in addition to the provision of free care through the Doctors of the World clinic and the creation of the Safe Surgeries GP toolkit, which enables GPs to circumvent the policies (Doctors of the World, 2019). Consequently, in May 2018 the terms of the MoU were suspended and its scope narrowed, permitting data sharing only in cases of serious criminal offences or risks to public security (NHS Digital, 2018). Finally, under threat of an imminent legal challenge from Migrants' Rights Network and Liberty arguing that the agreement 'violated patients' right to privacy, did not pass the considerable public interest test required to breach the doctor–patient relationship, left migrants too scared to access healthcare services, and discriminated against non-British patients' (Liberty, 2018) – in November 2018, NHS Digital withdrew entirely from the MoU (Bowcott, 2018). The Home Office has since announced its intention to work with NHS Digital on a new MoU (Bowcott, 2018). However, it will be established that due to its lack of legislative basis, unjustifiable impacts and clear conflict with medical ethics – such an agreement would only likely meet the same fate.

3. LACK OF LEGAL BASIS

Whilst not the main cause of action, the MoU's lack of legal basis was a clear factor in its perception as illegitimate and facilitated its straightforward withdrawal. Unlike most hostile environment policy, which is contained within legislation such as the *Immigration Act 2014 and 2016*, the MoU is 'not a contract nor is it legally binding' (Health and Social Care Committee, 2018a, Q135; MoU, 2017, para. 2.2), and this has repeatedly been cited as justification for NHS staff to disregard it (Doctors of the World, 2019; Health and Social Care Committee, 2018a). In contrast to the criminal sanctions imposed on employers and landlords

(*Immigration, Asylum and Nationality Act 2006*, s21; *Immigration Act 2016*, s35, s39), there was no penalty for failure to comply with the MoU, meaning a far more willing and open opposition could be built. The MoU *does* attempt to draw a 'legal basis' from *s261(5) of the Health and Social Care Act 2012* which allows for the disclosure of patient information in the public interest (MoU, 2017, para. 3.3). However, this had little impact on the MoU's credibility. Section 261(5) only confers a power and not an obligation (Health and Social Care Committee, 2018b, para. 35) to inform, and the MoU seemed to disregard s253(1)(ca) of the very same Act (*Health and Social Care Act 2012 as amended by the Care Act 2014,* s122(2)) which requires NHS Digital to have regard for 'the privacy of recipients of health services'. Moreover, NHS Digital's reliance (Wilkinson, 2019) on *W, X, Y and Z* ([2015] EWCA Civ 1034) to justify sharing addresses as 'low on the spectrum of confidential information' (*W, X, Y and Z* [2015] EWCA Civ 1034, para. 85) was viewed as 'unconvincing' and 'troubling' (Health and Social Care Committee, 2018b, para. 26) as the judgement clearly stated that this case must not be used as a 'Trojan horse' (*W, X, Y and Z* [2015] EWCA Civ 1034, para. 46) through which to dismantle the principle of confidentiality (Wollaston, 2018). Failure to consult with the medical profession is also likely to have reduced the MoU's credibility, leading to its perception as a 'backroom deal' (Liberty, 2018) particularly as healthcare is not the Home Office's area of expertise (Delamothe, 2012, p. 2). Consequently, the MoU was defied by NHS employees who sought instead to uphold their higher professional standards of confidentiality. In addition to limiting its legitimacy, the lack of legislation also enabled the MoU to be overturned in a straightforward manner. Unlike areas of the hostile environment enshrined in legislation, which would need to be expressly or impliedly repealed (Dicey, 1959; Elliott, 2003), the MoU was withdrawn simply through notice by NHS Digital (MoU, 2017, paras. 16–17). As such, the introduction of this policy through a MoU enabled a swifter and more straightforward withdrawal than had data sharing been introduced through legislation.

The significance of legislation may serve to explain why, despite sharing identical impacts and engaging the same ethical tensions, charging still remains in place. Charging policy has well established legislative roots reaching back to 1982 (*The National Health Service (Charges to Overseas Visitors) Regulations 1982*), and is now found in *s175 National Health Service Act 2006*, *s39 Immigration Act 2014*, and the *National Health Service (Charges to Overseas Visitors) Regulations 2015* which have since been amended by *The National Health Service (Charges to Overseas Visitors) (Amendment) Regulations 2017*. The very fact that the 'Patients not Passports' campaign against this policy has been in place since well before the MoU was even agreed, and yet charging has not yet been overturned, may illustrate the staying power that legislation affords these policies. However, within the space of two weeks the High Court has declared the 'Right to Rent' scheme discriminatory (*R (Joint Council For The Welfare Of Immigrants)* v. *Secretary Of State For The Home Department* [2019] EWHC 452 (Admin)) and suspended the 'Removal Notice Window' (*R (Medical Justice)* v. *Secretary of State for the Home Department* [2019] CO/543/2019). Whilst it is too soon to draw any firm conclusions, these decisions seem to represent a 'damning judgment' (Hill & Taylor, 2019) of the hostile environment, demonstrating why it 'must be dismantled' (High Court Suspends Home Office Deportations Policy, 2019; Hill & Taylor, 2019). These judgements do not affect the validity of hostile environment legislation, or alter the means by which legislation may be overturned, however, they certainly reduce the legitimacy with which these policies are perceived. If similar judgements continue, they may begin to undermine the entire premise of the hostile environment, leading to an increasing lack of credibility which may encourage further action to be taken.

4. EFFECTS

In this section, the impacts of data sharing and charging will be explored, with the aims of establishing how these motivated the action taken. Studies have shown patient circumstances to be the most influential factor in physician decision-making, (Dorr Goold, 2000) and as such, it is unsurprising that the following effects are recounted throughout the opposition as reasons for action. Medical professionals are uniquely positioned to interpret these effects due to their expertise, which arms them with an awareness of the significance of healthcare needs (Huddle, 2013), how these needs should be met (Huddle, 2013) and how policies may compromise patient care (Gruen, Pearson, & Brennan, 2004). This knowledge not only emphasises the severity of the hostile environment's impact in this area, but also enables physicians to act on and recount the effects of these policies with enhanced legitimacy, due to their professional authority in the area (Gruen et al., 2004). Both charging and data sharing carry the same impacts, and will therefore be dealt with together in this section unless indicated otherwise.

4.1. Impacts on Individual Patients

Contrary to NHS Digital's claims that usage of health systems will not be affected by these policies (Health and Social Care Committee, 2018a), a review of 66 studies revealed that national policies such as these are the number one barrier to healthcare, with fear of deportation identified as a barrier in 65% of studies (Hacker, Anies, Folb, & Zallman, 2015). Under the authority of PHE, the perceived or actual sharing of patient data 'has the potential to increase the number of documented and undocumented migrants who either delay or do not seek medical treatment' (PHE, 2017, p. 5). This has certainly been the case, with a clear loss of trust in the NHS leading individuals to avoid health services (Doctors of the World, 2017; PHE, 2017). In addition to loss of trust, inability to pay has caused 341 patients in an eight month period to decline treatment (Jayanetti, 2018), with countless others refraining from seeking care altogether (Duvell, Cherti, & Lapshyna, 2018). The deterrent effect is concerning for doctors who view it as 'imperative that healthcare services are allowed to be neutral, safe spaces that everyone in need of treatment can go to without … risk' (Savage & Cadwalladr, 2019). It is particularly concerning that, due to the culture of fear (Johnson, 2018) that has been created, even documented migrants have been deterred from healthcare (Equality and Human Rights Commission, 2018).

Lack of awareness surrounding the particulars of charging has led migrants to avoid care even in the most urgent of situations, despite emergency care being exempt from charges (*The National Health Service (Charges to Overseas Visitors) (Amendment) Regulations 2017*, Regulation 8 and 9). Nowhere is this issue more apparent than in antenatal care. Despite all maternity care being deemed immediately necessary (Department of Health and Social Care, 2019), almost two out of three pregnant migrant women avoid accessing antenatal care, with reports of women even presenting at hospital in labour having never sought antenatal care for fear of bills and deportation (Doctors of the World, 2017). Understandably, this has led physicians to characterise the policies as 'cruel' and 'inhumane' (Feldman, 2018).

Blanket fear of all health services may, however, be justified. Cases of urgent care being withheld due to mis-implementation of the charging regulations have been widely reported (Campbell, 2019), including the cases of Albert Thompson (Windrush Row: I was Denied NHS Cancer Treatment, 2018) and Elfreda Spencer (Jayanetti, 2018) who were both incorrectly denied cancer treatment. Poor implementation has not only led to unnecessary denial of treatment, but also discrimination: an effect that appears to have become the hallmark of the hostile environment (House of Commons Home Affairs Committee, 2018; Taylor, 2018). Doctors feel they are now 'expected to racially profile their patients' (Burn, 2018, p. 580) as confusion surrounding the various immigration statuses leads to ethnicity being used as a proxy for 'Britishness' (Achiume, 2018, paras. 37–38). It is due to this discriminatory impact that the UN Special Rapporteur on Discrimination has called for the repeal of all hostile environment policy (Achiume, 2018, para. 39). Therefore, considering this in conjunction with the Right to Rent case, it is possible that due to its wide applicability, discrimination may prove an important basis for action moving forward.

4.2. Broader Impacts

The MoU is justified on the basis of 'public interest' (MoU, 2017, para. 7.8), yet paradoxically also risks the health of the general public (Potter, 2017). PHE have warned that as a consequence of deterred health seeking behaviour, the public health of the wider community is also threatened due to the increased risk of transfer of communicable diseases (PHE, 2017). However, PHE's advice appears to have been comprehensively ignored (Wollaston, 2018). Whilst PHE are still consulting on the MoU's public health impacts (PHE, 2018), research suggests that deterred health seeking behaviour leads to increased risk of transmission of tuberculosis (Asch, Leake, & Gelberg, 1994; Martinez et al., 2015) and HIV (Dodds et al., 2008; Thomas, Aggleton, & Anderson, 2010). It is clear that these policies prioritise immigration objectives over important health objectives, and this is deeply concerning for the medical profession (Mosca, 2019; UCL-Lancet Commission, 2018).

Both the MoU and charging regulations rely on the economic justification of 'fair contribution' (Department of Health, 2017). This argument is based on the popular urban myth (Britz & McKee, 2015) of 'health tourism', which in reality only accounts for 0.3% of the NHS budget (Prederi, 2013). Over half of patients charged have not repaid their debt a year later (Doctors of the World, 2017) and as such, there appears to be little economic merit in chasing destitute migrants for bills they simply cannot pay by virtue of the very same hostile environment barring them from work. Restricting access to healthcare has, in fact, been shown to increase health expenditure by 40% compared to granting regular access (Bozorgmehr & Razum, 2015, p. 17), due to the higher costs associated with providing emergency care once the patient's condition has worsened (European Union Agency for Fundamental Rights, 2015). Continuing to restrict access to healthcare in this way will therefore only increase financial strain on the NHS. Moreover, the cost of implementing these policies is yet to be calculated and is likely to far outweigh any 'financial benefit' (Faculty of Public Health, 2018; Jayanetti, 2018; Jones, 2018). The policies have consequently been described by physicians as a 'merely punitive tool' (Potter, 2018), as their transparent lack of legitimate rationale only further intensifies the harshness of their effects.

This misleading economic rationale has also incited far broader concerns. It has been suggested that the 'health tourism' rhetoric is merely a means of scapegoating migrants for the underfunding of the NHS, which in reality is a result of austerity measures (Achiume, 2018; Fox & Hiam, 2018; Hiam et al., 2018; Russell, 2018). Doctors have expressed concern that labelling certain groups as 'undeserving' of NHS care (Potter, 2018) is a means of gradually privatising the NHS using an already marginalised group as the path of least resistance (Russell, 2018). It is therefore possible that the opposition is not only a response to the policies specifically, but also the threats these represent more broadly.

Therefore, it is clear that given their exposure to those affected by the policies, ability to interpret the wider implications, and vested interest in the future of the institution, NHS staff are ideally positioned to bear witness to these effects (Open Letter to Secretary of State for Health, 2017). By citing these experiences and statistics, physicians are able to ground their ethical objections (dealt with in the following section) in material harms (Potter, 2018) – thus fortifying their opposition as a whole. This holds much promise for action against charging, as these effects are common to both policies. However, this use of impacts may have limited application to other areas of the hostile environment where the effects are not so wide reaching and the actors do not hold as much expertise, or such a vested interest.

5. ETHICS

Ethical arguments have been central to both action against the MoU and the ongoing 'Patients not Passports' campaign. The opposition overwhelmingly views that 'the NHS's founding principles … and the duties of a doctor … have been eroded' (Burn, 2018, p. 580) by these policies, and uses the physician's ethical obligations as the main motivation for action. This section will explore two broad theories of healthcare ethics, these will then be used as a framework to give greater moral weight to the principles of the NHS. The physician's ethical obligations will also be examined in this way, and will be established as the main cause of action which served to unite physicians and provide the foundations for collective action.

5.1. Theories of Justice and Cosmopolitanism

Theories of justice are predominantly concerned with questions of resource distribution and are therefore employed in this area due to the MoU's impact on access to health services. Grounding itself in Rawls' 'Justice as Fairness' (2001), Daniels (1981, 2001) expands this theory to include healthcare as a primary good which should be protected due to its role in maintaining normal functioning, which in turn impacts equality of opportunity (Daniels, 1981, 2001). Whilst useful to highlight the importance of healthcare, Daniels' theory is limited by its reluctance to specify an exact distribution and failure to account for migrants specifically (Wild, 2015). Cosmopolitanism may be employed to address these shortcomings. Wild combines Daniels' view of access to healthcare as a primary good and Brock's cosmopolitanism – 'that every person ... is ... entitled to equal respect and consideration no matter what her citizenship status or other affiliations happen to be' (Brock, 2015, p. 112) – to argue that, as healthcare is so significant, it should be provided universally to all within a given jurisdiction (Wild, 2015) irrespective of 'morally arbitrary features such as immigration status' (Shahvisi, 2018, p. 340). Wild's theory goes so far as to argue that, states with sufficient resources, and which already provide universal healthcare to their citizens, have a 'moral obligation' (Wild, 2015, p. 166) to extend this care to all in their territory, due to the practicability of doing so (Wild, 2015). Having already established that charging and data sharing policies are based on a false economy (Russell, 2018), it is arguable that the UK is a state with one such moral obligation.

Whilst cosmopolitanism may seem nothing more than ideological, it in fact already operates within our healthcare system. The NHS is heavily reliant on staff from overseas and at present one in every eight NHS employees is a foreign national (Baker, 2018). In hiring these people, the NHS and government policy that permits their employment operates in an entirely cosmopolitan manner, considering only their qualifications without regard for their nationality (Shahvisi, 2018). This has been characterised as a 'partial cosmopolitanism' (Shahvisi, 2018, p. 335) as, in contrast, a patient's immigration status is central to their access to healthcare (Shahvisi, 2018). It is therefore apparent that cosmopolitanism may be achieved, albeit limited to situations that advantage the state (Shahvisi, 2018). It has been proposed that this biased cosmopolitanism should be corrected by extending universal healthcare to all migrants (Shahvisi, 2018), and it is even arguable on the basis of the evidence presented above, that this too would advance the state's interests with regard to public health and reducing strain on the NHS. Whilst this may be both ethically and evidentially substantiated, it is clear that neither ethics nor evidence are a factor in recent policy-making in this area.

5.2. Principles of the NHS

The NHS is regularly upheld as a shining example of universal healthcare and British values (Bhagawati, 2019; Russell, 2018). It is founded on three core principles: that 'it meets the needs of everyone, it is free at the point of delivery, and that it is based on clinical need, not ability to pay' (NHS, 2018). These principles can clearly be seen to project a cosmopolitan theory of healthcare distribution.

On creating the NHS, Bevan (2010) noted that 'it would be unwise as well as mean' to withhold care from migrants, yet this is precisely what is required by recent 'exclusionary' (UCL-Lancet Commission, 2018) policies that stand in direct conflict with these 'inclusive' (UCL-Lancet Commission, 2018) health goals. As such, it is clear why hostile environment policy has been characterised as 'inherently at odds with the founding ethos of the NHS' (Hiam & McKee, 2016, p. 228). Such views certainly assisted the opposition by enabling them to claim that not only their professional ethics, but the ethics of the institution as a whole were in jeopardy.

5.3. Professional Ethics

The predominant factor that incited physicians' action against the MoU is the incompatibility between the policy and their professional ethics. 'A gross violation of trust' (Potter, 2018), data sharing goes directly against ethical codes, such as The Hippocratic Oath (Lasagna, 1964), General Medical Council Guidance on Confidentiality (GMC, 2017), NHS Code of Practice on Confidentiality (Department of Health, 2003) and even NHS Digital's own Guide to Confidentiality in Health and Social Care (Health and Social Care Information Centre, 2013) which all emphasise confidentiality as the cornerstone of the medical profession (Doctors of the World and National Aids Trust, 2017). Unlike the absence of legislation which merely facilitated the action, or the MoU's effects which were cited to substantiate the opposition, ethics are directly referred to as the reason for mobilisation. Virtually all of the literature written by objectors draws on 'trust' and 'confidentiality' as the basis for action, with many explicitly citing the codes of ethics as their motivation (see, e.g., Bradley, 2018; Gulland, 2017, p. 1; Kmietowicz, 2018; Massey, 2018; McCall, 2017; Potter, 2018; Rimmer, 2017, p. 1). Of course, this confidentiality is not absolute and may be broken if in the public interest (GMC, 2017), but disclosures under the MoU go far beyond the exceptions permitted by the GMC (Doctors of the World and National Aids Trust, 2017). This tension between immigration and healthcare goals is no doubt a result of the failure to consult either medical professionals or ethicists before introducing the MoU (Health and Social Care Committee, 2018a), and illustrates why clinical perspectives are so essential in ensuring that the public interest in maintaining confidentiality is not overlooked (Caldicott, 2017). Contrary to Huddle's claim that 'social justice is a deeply contested notion' (Huddle, 2013, p. 370) for physicians, it is evident that these codes of ethics create a moral consensus based on shared values (Huddle, 2013). This alliance may have been facilitated by the NHS itself, which has been said to bind physicians together and created a 'greater collective awareness' (Cockerham, 1982; Jones, 1981). Ethics have therefore served as an integral factor in building an effective and united opposition to these policies, which enabled action to be brought collectively.

The centrality of ethical obligations may limit the applicability of this form of action to other areas of hostile environment policy. Adherence to such rigid codes of ethics appears to be unique to the medical profession, meaning that employers or landlords would not be able to simply transpose this form of action into their own profession. Nonetheless, Wild (2015) has emphasised that subscription to cosmopolitanism is not limited to health and could therefore be applied to other areas. This being said, it is doubtful that cosmopolitanism alone could provide a sufficient ethical basis for action. The significance of ethics does, however, promise much for the ongoing 'Patients not Passports' movement. This action is based on the same ethical objections, and is likely to have similar success due to the strength of these arguments, should the charging regime's legislative basis not prove too great a barrier.

5.4. Doctors' Public Role

Does it then follow that doctors *must* take action on this basis? Many physicians believe so, with over 90% rating community participation, political involvement, or collective advocacy as an important part of their profession (Gruen, Campbell, & Blumenthal, 2006). Opinions on precisely what this action should involve range from minor acts such as voting in elections (Gruen et al., 2004; Huddle, 2013) to the full spectrum of public interest advocacy (Gruen et al., 2004). Public interest advocacy is defined as 'the pursuit of influencing public policy and resource allocation decisions within systems and institutions that directly affect people's health' (Cohen, de la Vega, & Watson, 2001). This includes such acts as those taken against the MoU: raising public awareness, writing letters, signing petitions, forming groups for political advocacy, volunteering or offering free care (Gruen et al., 2004). These forms of action are especially regarded as falling within the physician's role due to their natural advocacy skills, special knowledge and proximity to health issues (Gruen et al., 2004) which grant them vast bargaining power (Pushkar, 2019, p. 248). Therefore, it appears that in addition to their ethical obligations, physicians have an obligation to address health-related issues, especially those concerning public health and barriers to healthcare (Gruen et al., 2006). Critics have sought to undermine this duty, claiming that social justice imposes requirements on physicians as *citizens* and not as *professionals* (Huddle, 2013). However, Pushkar (2019) is able to rebut these arguments by establishing that the responsibility is born out of a fusion of both professional *and* civic ethics, arguing that when professional ethics align with personal morals – politicised physicians emerge (Pushkar, 2019, p. 239). It is telling that politicians have criticised the profession as being 'too politicised' (Mclellan, 2018). Given that medical professionals rank as the most trusted profession, whilst politicians rank second to last (Ipsos MORI, 2018), this view may be a reflection of just how much power physicians yield in the political arena, as opposed to a substantive critique (Oliver, 2019, p. 1–2).

5.5. Collective Action

In order to defend their ethical obligations and fulfil their public roles, physicians not only joined together using their ethical codes, but joined forces with other stakeholders such as activists, NGOs and civil rights groups, to bring collective action against the MoU. The 'hallmark of professionalism' (Gruen et al., 2004, p. 97), collective action involves 'the joining together of individuals united by a common goal in order to consolidate power' (Dorr Goold, 2000, p. 498).

As explored above, it appears that physicians are already grouped by their shared ethical codes and NHS membership, however, it remains to be seen exactly how non-physician groups were engaged in this action. Jones' (1981) contends that collective action centres around the pursuit of a common 'collective good' (p. 3). Whilst a useful starting point, this theory is limited by its requirement that the 'collective good' be for the benefit of those taking action, namely physicians (Jones, 1981). Jones cannot account for our example which aimed to increase access to healthcare – a benefit for those *outside* of the medical profession, or how this goal was shared by medical and non-medical actors who do not represent one uniform group. Therefore, Dorr Goold's (2000) theory whereby 'collective action need not have as its only purpose the self-interest of the group' (p. 498) may better account for our example. By allowing for the pursuit of any 'common goals or interests', Dorr Goold (2000, p. 498) is able to account for goals beyond the interests of the medical profession, such as cosmopolitan access to healthcare. This in turn enables coalitions of collective action (Silberner, 2018) to be formed that span occupational groups (Pushkar, 2019, p. 242). Indeed, Dorr Goold (2000) argues that collective action proves most successful when its aims lie outside of the group's self-interests, as was the case against the MoU. Therefore, by taking action beyond the confines of the medical profession, and acting in an altruistic manner, physicians were able to strengthen their action.

It is therefore clear why the same collective action has been taken against charging. On the basis of its previous success against the MoU, there appears to be no better form of collective action for this purpose. As such, the action will likely prove successful, so long as the charging legislation does not restrict the success of further action. With regard to actors in other areas of the hostile environment, it appears that many of the possible goals of collective action would follow a more self-interested Jonesian framework, such as relieving administrative burden on employers or landlords (Lukes, Patel, & Peel, 2017; Sankey, 2013). As ethical arguments provide far stronger grounds for action, if actors in these areas were to oppose these policies, then a shift would be needed towards more morally weighted, selfless goals that mirror Goold's framework and therefore improve their chances of success.

6. FUTURE

Despite the dismantling of the MoU, it is clear that the hostile environment's grip on the NHS continues. Given the similarities between data sharing and charging policies, it is entirely logical that action has continued in the form of the 'Patients not Passports' campaign and it has been widely recommended that the charging regulations be withdrawn (Bradley, 2018; Doctors of the World, 2017; Feldman, 2018). Whilst this action is certainly gaining momentum, there are no signs of any such legislative change at present. As such, it has been suggested that a number of smaller steps should be implemented in the meantime to mitigate the harshness of the policy. Liberty has advised that the NHS commit to a firewall, whereby patient data will not be shared with the Home Office for the purposes of immigration enforcement (Bradley, 2018). This would prevent charging operating as a proxy for continued data sharing. Higher standards of staff training (Equality and Human Rights Commission, 2018), and removing the 50% surcharge (Feldman, 2018) on care would reduce the financial pressure the scheme imposes, and ensure that it is only applied when appropriate. These are all changes which would go a long way in improving patient care, should legislative change prove problematic. It has been suggested that following the Windrush scandal and Right to Rent case, the cracks in the hostile environment have begun to show (The Guardian View on the Hostile Environment, 2019; York, 2018). This optimistic view suggests that public opinion has shifted away from the xenophobic, anti-immigration rhetoric that has been cultivated in recent years, and that this provides an ideal climate in which to reject the hostile environment (York, 2018). This may well be the case, and the successful withdrawal of the MoU may serve as momentum for such action to continue. Public opinion is, however, notoriously fickle. As such, it would be more proactive to adopt changes such as improving the presence of health representatives within policy-making to ensure such damaging policies are not created in the first place (UCL-Lancet Commission, 2018; Wickramage & Annunziata, 2018), rather than relying on an unpredictable public opinion to oppose these policies once they have already been implemented. The hostile environment certainly holds less power than previously, and it is essential that movement against it continues. What form this movement takes and whether this will bring about any concrete changes, remains to be seen (York, 2018).

7. CONCLUSION

This chapter has sought to examine how the lack of legislative basis, wide reaching effects and ethical tensions of the MoU contributed to its withdrawal. It is clear that action was primarily incited by ethical arguments, which united physicians through their moral consensus, and provided the foundations for collective action with external actors. Whilst ethics were the focal point of the opposition, it is unlikely that the action would have succeeded on this basis alone. The wide ranging effects of the policy enabled these ethical objections to be grounded in visible harms, a factor which certainly strengthened the opposition. Although merely a facilitating factor and not a cause for action, the implementation of these data sharing duties through a MoU avoided the barrier of legislation – just how great an obstacle this poses will likely be revealed as the 'Patients not Passports' movement continues. Ethical arguments may have been the most prominent here, but it is not possible to conclude with any certainty that other factors were not also integral to the successful withdrawal of the MoU.

The success of the MoU's opposition may hold some telling lessons moving forward (Silberner, 2018). Whether action against charging proves successful may reveal if the MoU's opposition is in fact transferable, or limited to its precise context. Indeed, it appears that many of the contributing factors to its success: the wide reaching impacts, presence of ethical codes and authority of the profession, may already be limited to the context of the NHS. However, if we are truly moving towards a climate that fosters these anti-hostile environment sentiments, then perhaps action against other areas may not need such a comprehensive foundation. Due to the 'Patients not Passports' campaign comprising virtually identical action on the very same ethical grounds, it is likely that aside from its legislative basis, this action should prove equally successful. Likewise, should a new data sharing MoU be introduced, this would only likely meet the same fate. It has been made abundantly clear that discriminatory immigration policies are not welcome within the NHS and physicians will continue to oppose such schemes until their cosmopolitan goal of universal healthcare is achieved (Potter, 2018).

REFERENCES

Achiume, T. (2018). End of Mission Statement of the Special Rapporteur on Contemporary Forms of Racism, Racial Discrimination, Xenophobia and Related Intolerance at the Conclusion of Her Mission to the United Kingdom of Great Britain and Northern Ireland.

Asch, S., Leake, B., & Gelberg, L. (1994). Does fear of immigration authorities deter tuberculosis patients from seeking care? *Western Journal of Medicine*, *161*(4), 373–376.

Baker, C. (2018, October 10). *NHS staff from overseas: Statistics*. House of Commons Briefing Paper 7783. London: House of Commons Library.

Bevan, A. (2010). *In place of fear*. Whitefish, MT: Kessinger Legacy Reprints.

Bhagawati, D. (2019, February 17). My patient avoided NHS treatment for three years because he didn't want to become another Windrush Scandal Victim. *The Independent*. Retrieved from https://www.independent.co.uk/voices/nhs-health-windrush-jamaica-home-office-deportation-hostile-environment-a8783261.html

Bolt, D. (2019). *An Inspection of the Home Office (Borders, Immigration and Citizenship System) Collaborative with other Government Department Agencies*. Independent Chief Inspector of Borders and Immigration.

Bowcott, O. (2018, November 12). Home Office Scraps Scheme that used NHS Data to track migrants. *The Guardian*. Retrieved from https://www.theguardian.com/society/2018/nov/12/home-office-scraps-scheme-that-used-nhs-data-to-track-migrants. Accessed on November 14, 2018.

Bozorgmehr, K., & Razum, O. (2015). Effect of restricting access to health care on health expenditures among asylum-seekers and refugees: A quasi-experimental study in Germany, 1994–2013. *PLOS ONE*, *10*(7), 1–22.

Bradley, G. M. (2018). Care don't share. *Liberty*.

Britz, J. B., & McKee, M. (2015). Charging migrants for health care could compromise public health and increase costs for the NHS. *Journal of Public Health*, *38*(2), 384–390.

Brock, G. (2015). Global Justice, cosmopolitan duties and duties to compatriots: The case of healthcare. *Public Health Ethics*, *8*(2), 110–120.

Bulman, M. (2019, February 3). Home Office still using NHS patient data for immigration enforcement despite suggesting it would end practice. *The Independent*. Retrieved from https://www.independent.co.uk/news/uk/home-news/home-office-nhs-data-sharing-immigration-enforcement-a8761396.html

Burn, H. (2018). Returning our Ebola Medals: Our opposition to the hostile environment within the NHS. *British Journal of General Practice*, *68*(677), 580.

Campbell, D. (2019, February 17). Migrants wrongly told to pay for NHS care upfront, minister admits. *The Guardian*. Retrieved from https://www.theguardian.com/society/2019/feb/17/migrants-wrongly-told-to-pay-for-nhs-care-upfront-minister-says?CMP=Share_AndroidApp_WhatsApp

Care Act 2014.

Cockerham, W. C. (1982). Reviewed work(s): Doctors and the BMA: A case study in collective action by Philip R. Jones. *Contemporary Sociology*, *11*(6), 725–726.

Cohen, D., de la Vega, R., & Watson, G. (2001). *Advocacy for social justice: A global action and reflection guide*. Sterling, VA: Kumarian Press.

Daniels, N. (1981). Health-care needs and distributive justice. *Philosophy and Public Affairs*, *10*(2), 146–179.

Daniels, N. (2001). Justice, health and healthcare. *American Journal of Bioethics*, *1*(2), 2–16.

Delamothe, T. (2012). Migrant healthcare: Public health versus politics. *British Medical Journal*, *344*, 1–2.

Department of Health. (2003). *Confidentiality: NHS Code of Practice*. London: DH Publications. Retrieved from https://assets.publishing.service.gov.uk/government/uploads/system/uploads/attachment_data/file/200146/Confidentiality_-_NHS_Code_of_Practice.pdf

Department of Health. (2017). *Making a fair contribution*. London: Visitor & Migrant NHS Cost Recovery Programme. Retrieved from https://assets.publishing.service.gov.uk/government/uploads/system/uploads/attachment_data/file/590027/Cons_Response_cost_recovery.pdf

Department of Health and Social Care. (2019). Guidance on implementing the overseas. *Visitor Charging Regulations*.

Dicey, A. V. (1959). *Introduction to the study of the law of the constitution* (10th ed.). New York, NY: Macmillan & Co.

Doctors of the World. (2017). Deterrence, delay and distress: The impact of charging in NHS Hospitals on migrants in vulnerable circumstances. Retrieved from https://www.doctorsoftheworld.org.uk/wp-content/uploads/import-from-old-site/files/Research_brief_KCL_upfront_charging_research_2310.pdf

Doctors of the World. (2019). Safe Surgeries Toolkit. Retrieved from https://www.doctorsoftheworld.org.uk/wp-content/uploads/import-from-old-site/files/GP_toolkit_final.pdf

Doctors of the World and National Aids Trust. (2017). Briefing on the Memorandum of Understanding between Department of Health and the Home Office to Share Patient Information. Retrieved from https://www.doctorsoftheworld.org.uk/wp-content/uploads/import-from-old-site/files/Briefing_MOUwithHO_DOTW_NAT_2017_(3).pdf

Dodds, C., Hickson, F., Weatherburn, P., Reid, D., Hammond, G., Jessup, K., & Adegbite, G. (2008). *BASS Line 2007 Survey: Assessing the sexual HIV prevention needs of African people in England*. London: Sigma Research.

Dorr Goold, S. (2000). Collective action by physicians: Beyond strikes. *Cambridge Quarterly of Healthcare Ethics*, *9*, 498–503.

Duvell, F., Cherti, M., & Lapshyna, I. (2018). Does Immigration Enforcement Matter (DIEM)? Irregular immigrants and control policies in the UK. Final Report. Retrieved from https://www.compas.ox.ac.uk/wp-content/uploads/DIEM-Irregular-Immigrants-and-Control-Policies-in-the-UK.pdf

Editorial. (2019, March 3). The Guardian view on the hostile environment: The ‘Right to Rent’ and other wrongs. *The Guardian*. Retrieved from https://www.theguardian.com/commentisfree/2019/mar/03/the-guardian-view-on-the-hostile-environment-the-right-to-rent-and-other-wrongs?CMP=share_btn_tw

Elliott, M. (2003). Embracing ‘Constitutional’ legislation: Towards fundamental law? *Northern Ireland Legal Quarterly*, *54*(1), 25–42.

Equality and Human Rights Commission. (2018). *The lived experiences of access to Healthcare for People Seeking and Refused Asylum*. Research Report 122. Manchester, United Kingdom. Retrieved from https://www.equalityhumanrights.com/sites/default/files/research-report-122-people-seeking-asylum-access-to-healthcare-lived-experiences.pdf

European Union Agency for Fundamental Rights. (2015). *Cost of exclusion from Healthcare – The case of migrants in an irregular situation: Summary*. Luxembourg: Publications Office of the European Union. Retrieved from https://fra.europa.eu/sites/default/files/fra_uploads/fra-2015-cost-healthcare_en.pdf

Faculty of Public Health. (2018). *FPH briefing on the NHS charging regulations for overseas visitors in England*. Retrieved from https://www.fph.org.uk/media/2158/final-fph_briefing_nhschargingregs_1.pdf

Feldman, R. (2018). What price safe motherhood? Charging for NHS maternity care in England and its impact on migrant women. Retrieved from https://www.maternityaction.org.uk/wp-content/uploads/WhatPriceSafeMotherhoodFINAL.pdf

Fox, H., & Hiam, L. (2018). Migrant access to NHS Healthcare. *InnovAiT*, *11*(12), 693–698.

General Medical Council (GMC). (2017). *Confidentiality: Good practice in handling patient information*. Manchester, United Kingdom. Retrieved from https://www.gmc-uk.org/-/media/documents/gmc-guidance-for-doctors—confidentiality-good-practice-in-handling-patient-information—70080105.pdf?la=en&hash=08E96AC70CEE25912CE2EA98E5AA3303EAD B5D88 .

Grierson, J. (2018, August 27). Hostile environment: Anatomy of a policy disaster. *The Guardian*. Retrieved from https://www.theguardian.com/uk-news/2018/aug/27/hostile-environment-anatomy-of-a-policy-disaster

Gruen, R. L., Campbell, E. G., & Blumenthal, D. (2006). Public roles of US physicians. *Journal of the American Medical Association*, *296*, 2467–2475.

Gruen, R. L., Pearson, S. D., & Brennan, T. A. (2004). Physician-citizens – Public roles and professional obligations. *Journal of the American Medical Association*, *291*(1), 94–98.

Gulland, A. (2017). Handing NHS data to the Home Office. *British Medical Journal*, *356*, 1.

Hacker, K., Anies, M., Folb, B. L., & Zallman, L. (2015). Barriers to health care for undocumented immigrants: A literature review. *Risk Management and Healthcare Policy*, *8*, 175–183.

Health and Social Care Act 2012.

Health and Social Care Committee. (2018, March 15). *Oral Evidence: Memorandum of Understanding on Data-Sharing*. HC 677.

Health and Social Care Committee. (2018, April 15). Memorandum of Understanding on data-sharing between NHS Digital and the Home Office. Fifth Report of Session 2017-19. HC 677.

Health and Social Care Information Centre. (2013). A guide to confidentiality in health and social care.

Hiam, L., & McKee, M. (2016). Making a fair contribution: Is charging migrants for NHS care in line with NHS principles? *Journal of the Royal Society of Medicine*, *109*(6), 226–229.

Hiam, L., Steele, S., & McKee, M. (2018). Creating a 'hostile environment for migrants': The British Government's use of Health Service Data to restrict immigration is a very bad idea. *Health Economics, Policy and Law*, *13*, 107–117.

High Court Suspends Home Office Deportations Policy. (2019, March 21). Retrieved from https://ukhumanrightsblog.com/2019/03/21/high-court-suspends-home-office-deportations-policy/

Hill, A., & Taylor, D. (2019, March 1). Right to Rent Scheme ruled incompatible with Human Rights Law. *The Guardian*. Retrieved from https://www.theguardian.com/uk-news/2019/mar/01/right-to-rent-scheme-ruled-incompatible-with-human-rights-law

House of Commons Home Affairs Committee. (2018, January 15). *Immigration Policy: Basis for Building Consensus*. HC 500.

Huddle, T. S. (2013). The limits of social justice as an aspect of medical professionalism. *Journal of Medicine and Philosophy*, 38, 369–387.

Immigration Act 2014.

Immigration Act 2016.

Immigration, Asylum and Nationality Act 2006.

Ipsos MORI. (2018). Ipsos MORI Veracity Index 2018. Retrieved from https://www.ipsos.com/sites/default/files/ct/news/documents/2018-11/veracity_index_2018_v1_161118_public.pdf

Jayanetti, C. (2018, November 13). NHS denied treatment for migrants who can't afford upfront charges. *The Guardian*. Retrieved from https://www.theguardian.com/society/2018/nov/13/nhs-denied-treatment-for-migrants-who-cant-afford-upfront-charges

Johnson, E. (2018). Amending, suspending, unending: Sharing patient data and the journey of the MoU. Retrieved from https://www.doctorsoftheworld.org.uk/news/amending-suspending-unending-sharing-patient-data-and-the-journey-of-the-mou/?nabm=1&utm_referrer=https%3A%2F%2Ft.co%2F6yyyuihCsy

Jones, E. (2018, October 22). Upfront NHS charges one year on – 6 Reasons why they harm us all. *Open Democracy*. Retrieved from https://www.opendemocracy.net/en/ournhs/upfront-nhs-charges-one-year-on-6-reasons-why-they-harm-us-all/

Jones, P. R. (1981). *Doctors and the BMA: A case study in collective action*. Aldershot: Gower Publishing Company Limited.

Kmietowicz, Z. (2018). Doctors protest against 'Hostile Environment' Immigration Policy spreading to NHS. *British Medical Journal*, *361*, 1–2.

Lasagna, L. (1964). The Hippocratic Oath. Massachusetts, USA: School of Medicine, Tufts University. Retrieved from https://www.pbs.org/wgbh/nova/doctorsoath_modern.html#:~:text=Modern%20Version%20%7C%20PBS-,The%20Hippocratic%20Oath%3A%20Modern%20Version,those%20who%20are%20to%20follow

Legal Victory Against Government's Hostile Environment. (2018, November 12). Liberty. Retrieved from https://www.libertyhumanrights.org.uk/news/press-releases-and-statements/legal-victory-against-government%E2%80%99s-hostile-environment

Letter from Caldicott, F (2017, April 18) to Wollaston, S.

Letter from Massey, C (2018, January 12). Written Evidence from the General Medical Council. MOU0006.

Letter from Wilkinson, S (2019, February 23) to Wollaston, S.

Letter from Wollaston, S (2018, January 29) to Wilkinson, S.

Lukes, S., Patel, C., & Peel, C. (2017). The right to rent. *Journal of Immigration, Asylum and Nationality Law*, *31*(1), 51–69.

Martinez, O., Wu, E., Sandfort, T., Dodge, B., Carballo-Dieguez, A., Pinto, R., … Chavez-Baray, S. (2015). Evaluating the impact of immigration policies on health status among undocumented immigrants: A systematic review. *Journal of Immigrant and Minority Health*, *17*(3), 947–970.

McCall, B. (2017). UK NHS-Home Office Agreement undermines patient trust. *The Lancet*, *389*(10074), 18–24.

Mclellan, A. (2018, December 9). The Bedpan: The army takes values more seriously than the NHS. Retrieved from https://www.hsj.co.uk/comment/the-bedpan-the-army-takes-values-more-seriously-than-the-nhs-/7023972.article

Memorandum of Understanding Between Health and Social Care Information Centre and The Home Office and The Department Of Health, January 2017.

Mosca, D. T. (2019). The challenge of improving migrants' health: A way out of the quagmire? Retrieved from https://www.rcplondon.ac.uk/news/challenge-improving-migrants-health-way-out-quagmire?utm_source=Communications&utm_medium=email&utm_campaign=10279244_Commentary%20-%2017%20February%202019&utm_content=an%20abridged%20%EF%BB%BFarticle&dm_i=1V12,64BIK,DMKIAC,O1QJ2,1

National Health Service (Charges to Overseas Visitors) (Amendment) Regulations 2017.

National Health Service (Charges to Overseas Visitors) Regulations 1982.

National Health Service (Charges to Overseas Visitors) Regulations 2015.

National Health Service Act 2006.

NHS. (2018). Principles and values that guide the NHS. Retrieved from https://www.nhs.uk/using-the-nhs/about-the-nhs/principles-and-values/

NHS Digital. (2018). A statement from NHS Digital on the memorandum of understanding with the Home Office. Retrieved from https://digital.nhs.uk/news-and-events/latest-news/a-statement-from-nhs-digital-on-the-memorandum-of-understanding-with-the-home-office

Oliver, D. (2019). Can doctors be too politicised? *British Medical Journal*, *364*,1–2.

Open Letter to Secretary of State for Health. (2017, October 9). Withdraw the National Health Service (Charges to Overseas Visitors) (Amendment) Regulations 2017.

Partridge, N. (2014). Review of data releases by the NHS Information Centre. Retrieved from https://assets.publishing.service.gov.uk/government/uploads/system/uploads/attachment_data/file/367788/Sir_Nick_Partridge_s_summary_of_the_review.pdf

Potter, J. (2017). NHS urged to share data so patients can be deported. *The Conversation*. Retrieved from https://theconversation.com/nhs-urged-to-share-data-so-patients-can-be-deported-72380

Potter, J. (2018). Patients not passports – No borders in the NHS. *Justice, Power and Resistance*, *2*(2), 417–429.

Prederi. (2013). Quantitative assessment of visitor and migrant use of the NHS in England. Retrieved from https://assets.publishing.service.gov.uk/government/uploads/system/uploads/attachment_data/file/251909/Quantitative_Assessment_of_Visitor_and_Migrant_Use_of_the_NHS_in_England_-_Exploring_the_Data_-_FULL_REPORT.pdf

Public Health England (PHE). (2018). PHE call for evidence: Memorandum of understanding on data-sharing between NHS Digital and the Home Office. Retrieved from https://assets.publishing.service.gov.uk/government/uploads/system/uploads/attachment_data/file/694434/Call_for_evidence_26Mar18.pdf

Public Health England (PHE) Response to NHS Digital. (2017). National Back Office (NBO) Review. Retrieved from https://www.parliament.uk/globalassets/documents/commons-committees/Health/Correspondence/2016-17/Correspondence-Memorandum-Understanding-NHS-Digital-Home-Office-Department-Health-data-sharing.pdf

Pushkar, P. (2019). NHS Activism: The Limits and Potentialities of a New Solidarity, *Medical Anthropology*, 38(3), 239–252.

R (Joint Council For The Welfare Of Immigrants) v. *Secretary Of State For The Home Department* [2019] EWHC 452 (Admin).

R (Medical Justice) v. *Secretary of State for the Home Department* [2019] CO/543/2019.

Rawls, J. (2001). *Justice as fairness: A restatement*. Cambridge, MA: Harvard University Press.

Rimmer, A. (2017). BMA annual meeting: Department of Health must stop sharing patient details with Immigration Officers, says BMA. *British Medical Journal, 357,* -2.

Russell, N. (2018, April 8). Excluding migrants from the NHS undermines its founding principles. Red *Pepper*. Retrieved from https://www.redpepper.org.uk/excluding-migrants-from-the-nhs-undermines-its-founding-principles/

Sankey, I. (2013). Liberty's response to the Home Office Consultation on tackling illegal immigration in privately rented accommodation.

Savage, M., & Cadwalladr, C. (2019, February 16). Revealed: How Home Office hires out staff to hunt migrants. *The Observer*. Retrieved from https://www.theguardian.com/uk-news/2019/feb/16/home-office-hires-out-staff-hunt-migrants-hostile-environment?CMP=Share_iOSApp_Other

Shahvisi, A. (2018). Health worker migration and migrant healthcare: Seeking Cosmopolitanism in the NHS. *Bioethics*, *32*, 334–342.

Silberner, J. (2018, November 20). What happens when health care and immigration enforcement collide. *Politico Magazine*. Retrieved from https://www.politico.com/magazine/story/2018/11/20/health-care-immigration-enforcement-222640

Taylor, R. (2018, June 11). Impact of 'Hostile Environment' Policy Debate on 14 June 2018. House of Lords Library Briefing.

The Lancet Commission. (2018). The UCL-Lancet Commission on migration and health: The health of a world on the move. *The Lancet*, *392*, 2606–2654.

Thomas, F., Aggleton, P., & Anderson, J. (2010). "If I Cannot access services, then there is no reason for me to test": The impacts of Health Service charges on HIV testing and treatment amongst migrants in England. *AIDS Care*, *22*(4), 526–531.

W, X, Y and Z v. *Secretary of State for Health* [2015] EWCA Civ 1034.

Wickramage, K., & Annunziata, G. (2018). Advancing health in Migration Governance, and Migration in Health Governance. *The Lancet*, *392*(10164), 2528–2530.

Wild, V. (2015). Universal access to health care for migrants: Applying cosmopolitanism to the domestic realm. *Public Health Ethics*, *8*(2), 162–172.

Williams, S. (2018, December 20). Immigration White Paper: We treat #PatientsNotPassports. Retrieved from https://www.is21.org.uk/2018/12/20/immigration-white-paper-we-treat-patientsnotpassports/

Windrush Row: I was Denied NHS Cancer Treatment. (2018, April 18). *BBC News*. Retrieved from https://www.bbc.co.uk/news/av/uk-43818671/windrush-row-i-was-denied-nhs-cancer-treatment

York, S. (2018). The "Hostile Environment" – How Home Office Immigration Policies and Practices create and perpetuate illegality. *Journal of Immigration, Asylum and Nationality Law*, *32*(4), 363–384

CHAPTER 3

TWENTY-TWO YEARS OF EMPLOYER SANCTIONS: TO WHAT EXTENT HAS DEPUTISING EMPLOYERS WOVEN ETHNOCENTRISM INTO THE UK'S APPROACH TO CONTROLLING IRREGULAR MIGRATION?

Emily Rigler Gillingham

ABSTRACT

Since January 1997, the UK has imposed sanctions on employers found to be employing irregular workers. Coercing employers into conducting immigration status checks makes it increasingly difficult for irregular migrants to secure employment opportunities, thus restricting their ability to sustain a tolerable life in the UK. The deputisation of employers, as well as other private entities, such as landlords, has become a pivotal element of what is commonly known as the 'hostile environment', an attempt to make UK life unbearable for irregular migrants. This chapter uses the social science critique of ethnocentrism to explore different forms of bias and discrimination embedded in the deputisation of employers. Dehumanisation and exclusion are the two manifestations of ethnocentrism focussed on: examples of these recurring issues are drawn from the justifications for implementation, and effects of the employer sanctions regime.

Keywords: Employers; ethnocentrism; deputisation; hostile environment; sanctions; dehumanisation

Privatisation of Migration Control: Power without Accountability?
Studies in Law, Politics, and Society, Volume 86B, 41–56

ISSN: 1059-4337/doi:10.1108/S1059-433720210000086B004

1. INTRODUCTION

In December 1995, the House of Commons debated what would become the Asylum and Immigration Act 1996 (AIA 1996), s. 8, a provision introducing the first employer sanctions in the UK.[1] Suarez Congdon (2008) rightly identifies that the potential for ethnically charged discrimination during the policy implementation had dominated debate, with Diane Abbott highlighting 'immigration ... is always entangled with issues of race'.[2] The criminal sanctions came into force from 1997,[3] and were later bolstered by the civil penalties introduced under the Immigration, Asylum and Nationality Act (IANA) 2006.[4]

Whilst there is considerable contemporary journalistic and political debate surrounding the regime, there is less academic analysis: this chapter aims to contribute a 'law in context' interdisciplinary critique of the sanctions. Three main questions are examined: whether the foreshadowed discriminatory implementation proved correct; whether the sanctions introduced ethnocentrism or simply entrenched existing issues; and whether ethnocentrism extends beyond implementation into other parts of the policy process. A range of literature is used to answer these questions. Reports from non-governmental organisations are referenced, and whilst these are not peer-reviewed articles, they nevertheless provide valuable insight. To provide more grounded analysis where UK literature is unavailable, comparable resources are drawn from the United States, which has a more established employer sanctions regime.[5] Likewise, literature discussing the UK landlord sanctions scheme is used where appropriate, accounting for differences in employer–employee and landlord–tenant relationships.

The legal background to the sanctions is examined first, followed by the development of an ethnocentric framework to interrogate the regime. Specific examples are then used to trace ethnocentrism through the policy justification, policy implementation via the 'right to work' checks, and into policy effects, examining types of exclusion affecting irregular migrants.

2. BACKGROUND ANALYSIS

2.1. Legal Background

'Irregular' and 'undocumented' are used interchangeably to mean 'someone without the legal right to reside in the country s/he is in' (Valentine, 2010, p. 6), extending beyond irregular entrants to a broader category of individuals, including those who have overstayed or breached a visa, and refused asylum-seekers. In 2012, Theresa May announced her intention to create 'a really hostile environment for illegal migration' (as reported in Grierson, 2018), essentially to make life so intolerable for these individuals that they would voluntarily leave the UK.

This chapter focusses on the employer aspect of the hostile environment because employment is essential for survival, providing money required for housing, sustenance, and other pivotal goods and services. Valentine correctly identifies the significance of employment, writing that irregular migrants having a 'satisfying life' in the UK 'depended more than anything on employment' as 'there is no other way for them to have enough money to live on' (Valentine, 2010,

p. 5 & 23). Restricting employment makes it increasingly difficult for irregular migrants to sustain themselves, potentially 'forcing them to leave the country' (Bacon & Ong Hing, 2011, p. 85). The legal framework that deputises employers by establishing 'institutionalized partnerships [with] government authorities' (Walsh, 2014, p. 242), will now be briefly examined.

In addition to the original criminal offence of employing an irregular worker,[6] which carries a maximum five-year prison sentence,[7] there are multiple civil penalties issuable by notice (Home Office, 2019a, p. 6). The most significant is the penalty charge, which can total £20,000 per irregular worker (Home Office, 2019a, p. 9), although mitigating factors may reduce penalty sums (see Part V). A statutory defence to the penalty exists, which is exercisable only if the employer did not know of the illegality and 'shows that he complied with any prescribed requirements'.[8] Other civil penalties such as work closure notices,[9] and licence revocation[10] are also in effect.

2.2. Theoretical Background

This chapter critiques the sanctions regime using ethnocentrism, which narrowly envisaged is the perceived superiority of one's own ethnicity and culture. Smith (1972) accurately highlights the key notion that '[v]irtue and power belong ultimately to "my" group' (p. 10), whilst Baylor (2012) likewise identifies the 'cultural or ethnic bias' which 'often results in … value judgments that preference the in-group'.

Baylor (2012) rightly identifies ethnocentrism's evaluative worth, highlighting its status as a 'primary social critique' in anthropology, particularly in the 'era of globalization for those assuming their own cultural superiority'. Two key ethnocentric manifestations will be focussed on: dehumanisation and exclusion. Dehumanisation, defined by Haslam and Stratemeyer (2016) as 'the act of perceiving or treating people as if they are less than fully human' (p. 25), indicates ethnocentrism as believing the 'insider' group's superiority denigrates the relative status of the 'outsider'. As Utych (2018) accurately identifies, irregular migrants are 'prime targets of dehumanizing rhetoric' (p. 442). Systematic exclusion embodies ethnocentrism as it enforces separation based on the perceived inferiority of irregular migrants. These two elements are used to expose recurrent ethnocentrism engrained throughout the 22-year history of employer sanctions.

3. POLICY JUSTIFICATION

Ethnocentrism was evident before sanctions were introduced, with dehumanisation clearly manifesting in the policy justification. Migration control is commonly justified on security grounds, with Zembylas (2010) correctly noting immigrant 'figures are constructed … as being … strange and dangerous' with the potential to 'inflict[] serious damage on everyone else' (p. 39). The apparent threats extend beyond national security issues, and it is what Nyberg Sørensen (2012) labels 'non-traditional security threat[s] to cultural identity and social stability' that justify employer sanctions (p. 66). As Steele (2008) highlights the public perceives 'illegal immigration as a cause of crime and job displacement'

(p. 478), a sentiment shared during AIA 1996 parliamentary debates, with Baroness Blatch stating '[i]llegal working takes away jobs [from] people with a right to work here'.[11] The sanctions are thus seemingly legitimate security measures that defend the job and wage security of legal workers, by restricting irregular migrants gaining employment.

A key flaw of this migration–security nexus, is its ethnocentric tendency to focus on the protection and security of 'insiders', with Nyberg Sørensen (2012) rightly identifying the prioritisation 'of the West at the expense of the rest' (p. 67). Employer sanctions curtail safe and legitimate employment options, forcing irregular migrants into illicit employment with poor working conditions and wages (see Part V). As Ryan (2005) asserts, 'the growth in unauthorized work is associated with exploitative treatment by employers' (p. 28), so whilst legal workers may enjoy increased job and wage security, the security of irregular migrants is sacrificed. This deliberate subordination is justified by constructing the irregular migrant as threatening (Zembylas, 2010, p. 39), a dehumanising technique that presents the migrant as less worthy of protection than those legally in the UK. This is most effectively illustrated by the recurrent use of dehumanising labels in the public sphere. For instance, the Home Office guide explaining the sanctions to employers uses 'illegal worker[s]' and 'illegal working' eight times on the first page of substantive information (Home Office, 2014b, p. 3). Referring to irregular workers as 'illegal' reinforces their apparent criminality, constructing a barrier between 'us' as law-abiding 'insiders' in society, and irregular migrants as criminal 'outsiders' threatening 'our' employment and society. As Utych (2018) correctly highlights such dehumanisation excludes the targeted group 'from the typical moral consideration given to other[s]' as they 'are assigned lower levels of worth than non-dehumanized groups' (p. 441). The interests and safety of irregular migrants are thus smothered as inferior and undeserving, illustrating the ethnocentric prioritisation underpinning the regime.

4. POLICY IMPLEMENTATION

Prior to the introduction of sanctions, the potential for ethnically charged discrimination whilst employers implemented the regime was a pivotal concern. This chapter explores two ways this concern has been realised, grounding the discrimination in ethnocentrism.

4.1. Direct Discrimination

Much scholarship comments on the pervasiveness of ethnic conceptions of 'Britishness', which associates 'belonging' with ethnic characteristics (Heath & Tilley, 2005). The UN Special Rapporteur on Racism identified the discrimination such conceptions cause, stating 'white ethnicity confer[s] … presumed Britishness' on the holder (Tendayi Achiume, 2018, para. 38), whilst Ryan (2014) advances that employers will 'make assumptions about nationality from someone's appearance, accent, name' and related characteristics (p. 246). Deputising employers exposes job applicants to such conceptions of 'belonging', allowing employers to make ethnically charged decisions, whether intentionally or inadvertently. These assumptions can manifest in directly discriminatory treatment,[12] such as only checking documentation of ethnic minority applicants or not considering such applicants at all. The UN Special Rapporteur stressed this issue when noting 'ethnicity continues to be deployed in the public and private sector as a proxy for legal immigration status' (Tendayi Achiume, 2018, para. 38). Whilst her comments concern checking migration status generally, they nevertheless hold true for 'right to work' checks particularly, with the Home Office publishing a specific code of practice on avoiding race discrimination whilst conducting checks (Home Office, 2014a). The trend has also been identified in the United States, for example, in exploring discrimination against Latino workers, Bansak and Raphael (2001) identify the possibility that sanctions push employers to 'statistically discriminate against workers from ethnic groups disproportionately represented among the population of undocumented workers' (p. 277). Such discrimination embodies ethnocentrism as the 'outsider' group (ethnic minority applicants) is subjected to unfavourable treatment characterised by disproportionate scrutiny and intrusion.

These exact concerns were raised during AIA 1996 debates, with Jack Straw condemning the proposed sanctions on the basis employers would 'be scared away from taking any risk with … applicants with black or brown skins or foreign-sounding names'.[13] Likewise, in a leaked letter attacking the policy, former Minister Gillian Shephard expressed concerns 'that employers will concentrate checks on prospective employees whom they see as a risk, if not simply exclude them from consideration' potentially causing 'racial discrimination' (as reported in Victor, 1995).

Conversely, it is arguable that increasing the sanctions, as in 2014 when the maximum civil penalty doubled,[14] may promote equal treatment. Despite there being no legal duty to check every applicant's status, Bales (2017) rightly advocates that employers are 'compelled to … [conduct checks] in practice' (p. 281), as the sanctions make it precarious to conduct ad hoc checks based on appearance or accent. Only by conducting appropriate due diligence checks in the recruitment process does the statutory defence become available to employers,[15] thus conducting checks on all is the only way to protect against the sanctions.

However, whilst this may promote *de facto* equality, the law should be adapted to promote *de jure* equality: introducing a duty to check all job applicants would be an improvement, as it would indicate selectively implementing the policy, and thus potentially discriminating, is unacceptable. Additionally, as discussed next, ethnocentrism manifests not only in deciding which applicants to check, but also in determining which statuses to accept.

4.2. Indirect Discrimination

Deputised implementation also presents indirect opportunities for ethnically charged discrimination, caused by ethnocentric attitudes towards status. In attempting to avoid sanctions, some employers subcontract firms to check status on their behalf, a form of privatisation that Bloom (2015) classifies as 'indirect' and 'implicit' (p. 897). In assessing the regime, the Independent Chief Inspector of Borders and Immigration (ICIBI) noted the tendency of 'large UK-based businesses … to pay immigration advisers to check their "right to work" processes and records rather than rely on their in-house recruitment teams' (Bolt, 2015, p. 17), as a way to mitigate the sanctions risk and provide a defence.[16]

Cost prohibits this option for many businesses, and where checks are conducted in-house employers may be over-cautious, sticking to applicants with 'more secure immigration statuses' (Ryan, 2014, p. 248), such as British citizenship, which does not require document rechecks (Home Office, 2019b, p. 26). The House of Commons Home Affairs Committee, (2018) similarly reports instances

> of employers restricting access to job vacancies, for example by insisting that all non-EU applicants provide a biometric residence permit … or by limiting the vacancy to applicants with British passports. (p. 21)

Favouring more secure statuses naturally reflects ethnocentric priorities as employers select those with 'insider' status, such as British citizenship, over 'outsiders'. This prioritisation is similarly identified by the UN Special Rapporteur, who noted employers may 'err on the side of excluding all but those who can easily and immediately prove their Britishness' (Tendayi Achiume, 2018, para. 38), thus making the policy more exclusionary than the law requires, in line with ethnocentric attitudes.

Such practices cause indirect discrimination,[17] due to links between ethnicity and status. For instance, Ryan (2014) correctly highlights that preferring 'secure immigration statuses would tend to favour British and other EEA nationals' (p. 247), which will disproportionately advantage white groups. Despite imposing such preferences on all, employers risk indirectly discriminating as certain ethnic groups will benefit, whilst placing others at a 'particular disadvantage'.[18] This is likely to worsen as the hostile environment tightens: the tougher the sanctions, the more employers will try to avoid them, implementing increasingly exclusionary practices to avoid risk.

However, it must be noted that discrimination in policy implementation predates the sanctions regime: racist allegations permeate all migration control, including non-deputised functions. For instance, workplace raids conducted by Immigration Enforcement (IE) disproportionately target South Asian food outlets (Corporate Watch, 2016). Corporate Watch (2016) aptly distilled the racialised effects of this when stating 'people from Pakistan, Bangladesh and India make up 75% of those arrested'. ICIBI highlighted this as an area for improvement, pertinently noting the current trend in raid targets is 'self-reinforcing and limiting in terms of … the nationalities encountered. Other business sectors and possibly other nationalities had been neglected by comparison' (Bolt, 2015, p. 5). This illustrates that even IE produces discriminatory trends, and thus deputising employers has not introduced ethnically charged discrimination into irregular migration control.

That being acknowledged, it is likely deputised migration control is more discriminatory along ethnoracial lines than policy implemented by IE. This can be attributed to two key factors: available knowledge and threat of sanctions. Firstly, employers are not IE officers, and are likely to possess less information about which statuses satisfy 'right to work' requirements. As memorably encapsulated by Stuart McDonald in relation to the landlord sanctions: '[w]e are setting off down a road of amateur immigration control'.[19] A parallel can be drawn as both employers and landlords are amateur in the sense of not being IE officers. Additionally, employers are threatened by sanctions, and are therefore more likely to act cautiously to avoid penalties.

These factors distort policy implementation in a more exclusionary manner than checks conducted by IE. When IE is involved in workplace raids, they possess the relevant knowledge and are not threatened by sanctions, so make accurate status determinations. Comparatively, the cautious employer who restrictively implements the policy, may exclude individuals who are entitled to work. This exclusionary tendency is an acknowledged result of the United States employer regime, with Bacon and Ong Hing (2011) emphasising that approximately '430,000 employers only hired applicants born in the United States or did not hire applicants with temporary work documents in order to be cautious' (Bacon & Ong Hing, 2011, p. 87). Whilst relating to the United States, it is informative that the same pattern has been identified with the UK landlord sanctions regime. For instance, JCWI rightly captures direct and indirect discrimination:

> 42% of landlords said that the Right to Rent requirements have made them less likely to consider someone who does not have a British passport. 27% are reluctant to engage with those with foreign accents or names. (The Joint Council for the Welfare of Immigrants, 2015, p. 37)

In *R (JCWI)*, Mr Justice Spencer confirmed 'landlords are discriminating against potential tenants on grounds of nationality and ethnicity ... because of the Scheme', consequently declaring its incompatibility with the European Convention on Human Rights (*R (JCWI)* v. *Home Secretary*, 2019, paras. 93 & 134). Whilst further research into the effects of the UK employer regime is required, both the UK landlord sanctions and the US employer sanctions tentatively confirm Bloom's proposal that '[p]rivate actors play an increasing role in ... creating or perpetuating exclusions' (Bloom, 2015, p. 892). Ultimately therefore, deputisation likely results in more *de facto* exclusionary implementation in line with ethnocentric conceptions of belonging. Thus, whilst deputising employers did not introduce ethnocentrism into policy implementation, it has worsened its impact.

5. POLICY EFFECTS

Space precludes discussion of all the regime's exclusionary effects, so four examples are selected to illustrate how ethnocentrism manifests in different forms. The types of exclusion are often interlinked and reinforcing, but have been separated for clarity.

5.1. Social Exclusion

Levitas et al. (2007) succinctly encapsulate the core of social exclusion when stating it includes 'the inability to participate in the normal relationships and activities, available to the majority' (p. 9), with Mack (2016) similarly emphasising it as an impediment to flourishing 'relationships with others'. Employer sanctions have facilitated social exclusion by distorting relationships in two crucial ways. Firstly, removing the right to work denies irregular migrants the integration granted by employment. Although the regime does not actually stop irregular migrants working, see *Economic Exclusion*, it does push them into the shadow economy. The need to stay 'invisible' (Valentine, 2010, p. 39), denies irregular migrants what Nessel (2015) identifies as employment's 'transformative' potential, which provides 'a sense of belonging to a community [that] is essential to one's sense of place in the world' (p. 314). Aycan and Berry (1996) particularly highlight the fundamental connection between social interaction during employment and the adaptation to the host society it facilitates. Employer sanctions thus smother the integration of irregular migrants, cementing the divide between irregular migrants and society. The enforced separation ethnocentrically denigrates irregular migrants, denying what Nessel (2015) terms the 'sense of identification and value' associated with work in a dehumanising manner (p. 314).

Exclusion is heightened by the fact precarious 'undocumented' status typically results in irregular migrants working and living entirely within their own homogeneous ethnic communities, notably because of the sense of security offered by the group. Bloch (2013) accurately identifies this causes a form of secondary social exclusion, as 'working within the ethnic economy can limit access to participation in the wider society' (p. 275).

In addition to exclusion in the abstract sense, the sanctions also irrevocably change the employer–employee relationship. An adversarial edge is created by embedding migration control in the relationship, as employers have interests (avoiding sanctions) that are contrary to the interests of irregular migrants (working). For instance, civil penalty sums can be reduced by £5,000 if the employer reports 'suspected illegal workers', plus another £5,000 deduction for 'active cooperation' with IE (Home Office, 2019a, p. 12). Likewise, 'Operation Skybreaker' represents IE's 'shift … towards … greater engagement with businesses' (Bolt, 2015, p. 4), by collaborating with employers. Such tactics represent the increasing installation of control and fear in employer–employee relationships, with Bales (2017) rightly explaining the regime results in employers being 'incentivized' to betray workers, even when they 'have no legal duty to expose their staff' (p. 288). The Byron Burgers sting is illustrative of this distorted relationship, with Byron calling employees into work for what Bales (2017) labels as 'arrest by appointment' (p. 279). Likewise, in relation to the sanctions levied on Tesco, Hough (2012) reported IE approached Tesco and 'asked them to keep giving the students illegal overtime "in order to catch them in the act" '. Such collaboration fundamentally undermines the employer–employee relationship of mutual trust and confidence (*Malik* v. *BCCI*, 1997), replacing it with an alliance with IE. Indeed, this concern was voiced before sanctions were introduced, with Lord Lester highlighting the emerging 'culture of suspicion between employer and employed'.[20]

This policy exacerbates social exclusion and isolation due to a mutual perception change of the 'other' group. Irregular migrants may distance themselves from employers and wider society, perceiving them as informants. Conversely, employer collaboration presents irregular migrants as requiring surveillance, another dehumanising technique that presents migrants as threatening.

5.2. Legal Exclusion

The sanctions moved immigration 'gatekeepers' into the workplace, excluding irregular migrants from the right to work. This legitimises discrimination as it mandates divergent treatment based on immigration status: some individuals enjoy the right, whilst others do not. By denying rights and permitting discrimination, the law institutionalises the dehumanising rhetoric that irregular migrants are undeserving and worth less than everyone else. As Bacon and Ong Hing (2011) accurately assert, as 'laws are enforced, they are accepted as common practice' (p. 95), meaning they entrench the dehumanising perception that irregular migrants are not worthy of rights and protections that 'insiders' enjoy. This rhetoric is especially apparent when considering the other rights removed from irregular migrants as part of the hostile environment, such as the right to rent.[21]

The Supreme Court had the opportunity to mitigate discriminatory effects using the Equality Act 2010 (EA 2010) in *Taiwo* v. *Olaigbe* (2016), but instead of expansively interpreting 'race' to protect those discriminated against because of immigration status, it was held immigration status should remain a separate category. As Bales (2017) rightly concludes the effect is that '[e]mployees ... targeted in the workplace on the basis of their immigration status ... [cannot] make any claim' under EA 2010 (p. 285).

The hostile environment policies, including the employer regime, wrongly assume everyone can prove status, which has caused the wrongful legal exclusion, and thus legitimised discrimination, of 'blameless individuals settled in the UK legally' (Bawdon, 2014, p. 29). The UN Special Rapporteur specifically noted the hostile environment's place 'at the center of ... the Windrush scandal' (Tendayi Achiume, 2018, para. 33), which provides a contemporary case study of wrongful legal exclusion. When many of the Windrush generation arrived in the UK, they did so legally but without documentation which was not required at the time. This lack of paperwork meant many could not prove status to the deputised gatekeepers, resulting in discrimination when accessing employment and other services. A whole generation of Caribbean descendants may have been misclassified and caught up in the hostile environment checks due to the retrospective effect, resulting in legal exclusion.

5.3. Economic Exclusion

Superficially, restricting the right to work prevents irregular migrants from gaining employment, thus reducing the 'pull-factors' for immigration. However, many commentators rightly note this is inaccurate. Bloch, Kumarappan, and McKay (2015) indeed identify the opposite, noting the introduction of sanctions was followed by an increase in undocumented migration. Likewise, Brownell (2017) highlights an analogous pattern in the United States which suggests 'employer sanctions provisions ... failed to create disincentives to the hiring and employment of unauthorized immigrants' (p. 88). Instead, the regime has changed the nature of work undertaken, pushing irregular migrants into predominantly undesirable work with a number of recurring characteristics. Firstly, work opportunities are usually secretive, or in the hidden economy. Bloch et al. (2015) correctly identify employer sanctions as a factor in causing irregular migrants to turn 'to informal work where they are more vulnerable and more hidden' (p. 136). The work often involves poor working environments, with McKay and Wright (2008) concluding 'the more precarious a worker's status, the more dangerous the jobs they were doing' (p. 659). Work is typically low-paid, often less than minimum wage, as anecdotally noted in *East Lindsey District Council* (2016, para. 3).

Poor working conditions are common because of the power imbalance in employer–employee relationships, meaning irregular migrants cannot complain about conditions. There are multiple explanations for Bloch's sobering observation that the cost of work for irregular migrants is 'hav[ing] to accept what is offered' (Bloch, 2013, p. 282).

Firstly, the sanctions have drastically limited employment opportunities for irregular migrants. Reputable employers comply with regulations and conduct checks, thus pushing irregular migrants from the traditional labour market towards unscrupulous employers willing to break the law. Precarious 'undocumented' status makes it very difficult to challenge employers on poor working conditions or wages. As Dwyer, Lewis, Scullion, and Waite (2011) rightly state, '[i]mmigration status may operate to reduce the bargaining power for the worker to negotiate terms and conditions of employment or to escape an exploitative working environment' (p. 21). Employers use their power to threaten workers, for example, with dismissal or exposure to authorities. Corporate Watch (2016) provides prominent examples of the latter, highlighting that Deliveroo, Amey and ISS staff were all subject to 'employer-supported raids' whilst 'involved in [employment] disputes'. Treating irregular workers as disposable is inherently dehumanising, promoting the idea that irregular migrants should accept what is offered, and be penalised for seeking more.

Likewise, it is difficult for irregular workers to enforce labour rights judicially. Axiomatically, initiating a claim would attract unwanted attention from the authorities and IE. However, even if the migrant wanted to initiate a challenge, *ex turpi causa* may block the claim anyway. Despite the recent relaxation of doctrine (*Patel* v. *Mirza*, 2016), Fellows (2016) correctly asserts a degree of uncertainty remains meaning '[e]ach case will … turn on its facts'. Bales (2017) highlights several factors that would harm the case of irregular migrants, correctly identifying the risk that public policy reasons may 'endorse the strict application of the illegality doctrine' (p. 284), meaning the illegal nature of the migrant's employment contract would block a claim. Uncertainty surrounding the doctrine's current formulation, plus the costs and attention of bringing a claim, makes enforcing rights against an employer an unlikely option. Bloch (2013) accurately advocates the effect is that employers can 'circumvent statutory employment rights such as the minimum wage, health and safety provisions and holiday and sick pay' (p. 274).

In the United States, an alternative proposition outlining how sanctions contribute to poor working conditions is grounded on the ability of employers to shift the burden of sanctions onto workers. Massey and Gentsch (2014) advocate employers 'transfer[] the costs and risks of [employing irregular workers] … to the workers themselves' through low wages and standards (p. 496), with Bansak and Raphael (2001) adding this 'compensate[s] employers for undertaking the risk of … fines' (p. 276). For employers, there must be some additional benefit from hiring irregular workers to offset the risk of sanctions, and this theory suggests benefit comes via reduced costs from lower wages and poor working conditions. Again, the power imbalance means workers are effectively powerless to challenge the risk they bear. Hence, increasing sanctions could further reduce irregular migrant wages and working conditions, to offset increased risk for employers.

Whichever theory is preferred, ethnocentric dehumanisation remains at its core. Forcing irregular migrants to work in sub-standard conditions for low wages that would be unacceptable for legal workers, re-enforces their 'less worthy' status. This type of work is undertaken by most irregular migrants, regardless of education or skill level. In Valentine's (2010) research, she highlights that '[o]nly two ... participants had ever been able to use their professional qualifications' whilst '[f]ourteen had post-school qualifications from home', thus irregular migrants are 'highly likely to be under-employed, technical or professional qualifications unused as they carry out the low-paid, low-status jobs available' (p. 3 & 44). As succinctly captured by Global Future Council on Migration (n.d.), this embodies and facilitates the ethnocentric expectation that irregular migrants are 'to enter the labour market from the bottom', below legal workers in the very worst jobs.

5.4. Psychological Exclusion

Systematic exclusion psychologically impacts irregular migrants, particularly regarding self-worth: the dehumanisation becomes internalised. Valentine (2010) particularly links the regime with '[t]he shame of no longer being able to support the family at home, [which] can contribute to depression and anxiety' (p. 44). Similarly, Khosravi (2007) interestingly advances the point in his reflective article: 'the illegal migrant, subjected to a gaze and treatment that divests him or her of humanity, internalises the shame' equating irregular status with 'personal deficiencies and inadequacies' (p. 331).

An intriguing parallel can be drawn to Agamben's camp dehumanisation theory, where inhabitants are 'stripped of every political status and wholly reduced to bare life' which results in individuals 'from whom humiliation, horror, and fear had so taken away all consciousness and all personality' (Agamben, 1998, p. 171 & 185). Similarities exist between Agamben's camp inhabitants, who are degraded and dehumanised to breaking point, and irregular migrants who are likewise dehumanised, stripped of rights, and subsequently excluded. Even when not held in camps, dehumanisation psychologically damages irregular migrants in a way that distorts self-perception. One of Bawdon's (2014) interviewees encapsulates such self-depreciation: '[i]f the state says you have no status ... [y]ou are absolutely nobody. You can't stand up and speak' (p. 30). Irregular migrants can become so degraded and distraught that they do not value themselves properly, which leads to issues of modern slavery including forced labour.[22]

This unsavoury phenomenon is illustrated by the Vietnamese women enslaved in nail bars across the UK. For instance, one newspaper reported two undocumented Vietnamese girls working '60 hours a week' in a nail bar, in which '[o]ne was being paid about £30 a month while the second was not paid' (Morris, 2018). Dwyer et al. (2011) correctly highlight the link between irregular status and forced labour, explaining that '[w]ith few legal rights to residence, work or welfare, irregular migrants are likely to be the group most vulnerable to forced labour' (p. 16). But it is not just the legal exclusion of irregular migrants that makes them especially vulnerable. As Caroline Haughey QC rightly notes in response to questioning a forced labour victim, '[the victim's] view of herself is that she doesn't matter' (as included in BBC, 2018, at 46:59). The ethnocentric dehumanisation the employer sanctions contribute to is internalised by the irregular migrant, leading to feelings of inferiority and irrelevancy. Unsurprisingly the Modern Slavery Helpline identified modern slavery 'is normally more prevalent among the more vulnerable or within … socially excluded groups' (Modern Slavery Helpline, publication date unavailable, p. 18), indicating the exacerbated exclusion caused by employer sanctions facilitates exploitation.

Ironically, modern slavery victims often become trapped in the UK in an excluded underclass. The hostile environment means many victims feel so invisible and isolated they cannot reach out for help, and thus have no alternative but to stay with their captors, encapsulated by Caroline Haughey QC as 'incarceration by lack of choice, because there is no alternative' (as included in BBC, 2018, at 25:45). Ultimately therefore, the hostile environment traps the most vulnerable in the UK, subverting its purpose of encouraging voluntary deportation.

6. CONCLUSION

Since before the first employer sanctions were introduced, debate has centred on the potential for discrimination. However, ethnocentrism is found in more than just discriminatory implementation of the policy, and can be traced into the policy justification and effects. This chapter has sought to demonstrate the extent to which ethnocentrism permeates the regime using lenses of dehumanisation and exclusion.

Undoubtedly, employer sanctions constitute a salient instrument of the hostile environment, considering employment can be the difference between a satisfying life and abject destitution. This, coupled with the extensive amounts of journalistic and political debate, make it surprising the UK's employer regime has not attracted more academic analysis. Particularly valuable would be the application of critical lenses other than ethnocentrism, and an examination of possible reforms, both of which are unfortunately beyond the scope of this chapter.

Almost a year has passed since Home Secretary Sajid Javid supposedly disowned the 'hostile environment' in favour of a 'compliant environment' (Poole, 2018). However, as the UN Special Rapporteur rightly highlighted, '[s]hifting … the rhetoric … will have little effect if the underlying legislative framework remains intact' (Tendayi Achiume, 2018, para. 38). Despite there being no explicit attempts at repeal or reform of the employer regime, the cracks in the wider hostile environment are beginning to show. Following the Windrush scandal, Immigration Minister Caroline Nokes announced the Home Office was 'providing additional support to … employers' and encouraging them 'to get in touch with the Home Office checking service if a Commonwealth citizen does not have the documents they need'.[23] Moreover, the High Court delivered a significant blow to the hostile environment in its March decision to declare the landlord sanctions regime incompatible with the ECHR (*R (JCWI)* v. *Home Secretary,* 2019). Notably, Mr Justice Spencer stated 'any scheme of this kind will inexorably lead landlords down the path of discrimination and operate in a way which is incompatible with Article 14 ECHR' (*R (JCWI)* v. *Home Secretary,* 2019, para. 127). In asserting her disappointment with the decision, Nokes stated the Home Office was 'granted permission to appeal all aspects of the judgment', adding that for the time being, landlord sanctions continue to operate.[24] In light of such developments, one hopes the government recognises the problems caused by deputising private individuals, and addresses the lessons of ethnocentrism embedded in the past 22 years of employer sanctions.

NOTES

1. HC Debate. (1995, December 11). vol 268, col 699.
2. HC Debate. (1995, December 11). vol 268, col 767.
3. Asylum and Immigration Act 1996 (Commencement No 3 and Transitional Provisions) Order 1996, SI 1996/2970.
4. Immigration, Asylum and Nationality Act 2006, s. 15.
5. Immigration Reform and Control Act 1986.
6. Immigration, Asylum and Nationality Act 2006, s. 21.
7. Immigration Act 2016, s. 35(4).
8. Immigration, Asylum and Nationality Act 2006, s. 15(3).
9. Immigration Act 2016, sch 6.
10. *East Lindsey District Council* v. *Abu Hanif* [2016] EWHC 1265 (Admin), [2016] 4 WLUK 301.
11. HL Debate. (1996, March 14). vol 570, col 1009.
12. Equality Act 2010, s. 13(1).
13. HC Debate. (1995, December 11). vol 268, col 720.
14. Immigration (Employment of Adults Subject to Immigration Control) (Maximum Penalty) (Amendment) Order 2014, SI 2014/1262.
15. Immigration, Asylum and Nationality Act 2006, s. 15(3).
16. Immigration, Asylum and Nationality Act 2006, s. 15(3).
17. Equality Act 2010, s. 19(1).
18. Equality Act 2010, s. 19(2)(b).
19. HC Debate. (2015, October 1). vol 600, col 218.
20. HL Debate. (1996, March 14). vol 570, col 975.
21. Immigration Act 2014, s. 21.
22. International Labour Organisation CO29 Forced Labour Convention 1930, art 2(1).
23. HC Debate. (2018, July12). vol 644, col 1113.
24. HC Debate. (2019, March 5). vol 655, col 30WS.

Bibliography

Primary Sources

Statutes and Statutory Instruments

UK

Asylum and Immigration Act 1996.

Asylum and Immigration Act 1996 (Commencement No 3 and Transitional Provisions) Order 1996, SI 1996/2970.

Equality Act 2010.

Immigration Act 2014.

Immigration Act 2016.

Immigration, Asylum and Nationality Act 2006.

Immigration (Employment of Adults Subject to Immigration Control) (Maximum Penalty) (Amendment) Order 2014, SI 2014/1262.

USA

Immigration Reform and Control Act 1986.

Cases

East Lindsey District Council v. *Abu Hanif* [2016] EWHC 1265 (Admin), [2016] 4 WLUK 301.

Malik v. *Bank of Credit and Commerce International (BCCI); Mahmud* v. *Bank of Credit and Commerce International* [1997] UKHL 23, [1998] AC 20.

Onu v. *Akwiwu and another; Taiwo* v. *Olaigbe and another* [2016] UKSC 31, [2016] 1 WLR 2653.

Patel v. *Mirza* [2016] UKSC 42, [2017] AC 467.

R (Joint Council for the Welfare of Immigrants) v. *Secretary of State for the Home Department [2019] EWHC 452 (Admin),* [2019] 3 WLUK 12.

Tinsley v. *Milligan* [1994] 1 AC 340 (HL).

International Treaties

International Labour Organisation CO29 Forced Labour Convention 1930.

Hansard

HC Debate. (1995, December 11). vol 268, col 699.

HC Debate. (1995, December 11). vol 268, col 720.

HC Debate. (1995, December 11). vol 268, col 767.

HL Debate. (1996, March 14). vol 570, col 975.

HL Debate. (1996, March 14). vol 570, col 1009.

HC Debate. (2015, October 1). vol 600, col 218.

HC Debate. (2018, July12). vol 644, col 1113.

HC Debate. (2019, March 5). vol 655, col 30WS.

Secondary Sources

Agamben, G. (1998). *Homo Sacer: Sovereign power and bare life*. Stanford, CA: Stanford University Press.

Aycan, Z., & Berry, J. W. (1996). Impact of employment-related experiences on immigrants' psychological well-being and adaptation to Canada. *Canadian Journal of Behavioural Science*, *28*(3), 240–251.

Bacon, D., & Ong Hing, B. (2011). The rise and fall of employer sanctions. *Fordham Urban Law Journal*, *38*(1), 77–105.

Bales, K. (2017). Immigration raids, employer collusion and the Immigration Act 2016. *Industrial Law Journal*, *46*(2), 279–288.

Bansak, C., & Raphael, S. (2001). Immigration reform and the earnings of Latino workers: Do employer sanctions cause discrimination? *Industrial and Labor Relations Review*, *54*(2), 275–295.

Bawdon, F. (2014, October). *Chasing status: If not British, then what am I?* London: Legal Action Group.

Baylor, E. (2012, January 11). Ethnocentrism. Retrieved from http://www.oxfordbibliographies.com/view/document/obo-9780199766567/obo-9780199766567-0045.xml#obo-9780199766567-0045-div2-0001

BBC. (2018, August 9). The Prosecutors: Modern day slavery. Retrieved from https://www.bbc.co.uk/programmes/b0bfdn7h

Bloch, A. (2013). The labour market experiences and strategies of young undocumented migrants. *Work, Employment and Society*, *27*(2), 272–287.

Bloch, A., Kumarappan, L., & McKay, S. (2015). Employer sanctions: The impact of workplace raids and fines on undocumented migrants and ethnic enclave employers. *Critical Social Policy*, *35*(1), 132–151.

Bloom, T. (2015). The business of noncitizenship. *Citizenship Studies*, *19*(8), 892–906.

Bolt, D. (2015, December). An inspection of how the Home Office tackles illegal working. Retrieved from https://assets.publishing.service.gov.uk/government/uploads/system/uploads/attachment_data/file/547674/ICIBI-Report-on-illegal-working-December_2015.pdf

Brownell, P. (2017). Employer sanctions and the wages of mexican immigrants. *The Russell Sage Foundation Journal of the Social Sciences*, *3*(4), 70–96.

Corporate Watch. (2016, August 30). Snitches, stings and leaks: How immigration enforcement works. Retrieved from https://corporatewatch.org/snitches-stings-leaks-how-immigration-enforcement-works-2/#

Dwyer, P., Lewis, H., Scullion, L., & Waite, L. (2011, October). *Forced labour and UK Immigration Policy: Status matters?* York: Joseph Rowntree Foundation and University of Salford.

Fellows, B. (2016, October 3). Illegality as a defence to a Civil Claim (*Patel* v. *Mirza*). Retrieved from http://www.dlapiper.com/en/uk/insights/publications/2016/10/banking-disputes-quarterly/illegality-as-a-defence-to-a-civil-claim/

Global Future Council on Migration. (n.d.). A role for the private sector in 21st century Global Migration Policy. Retrieved from https://gfmdbusinessmechanism.org/wp-content/uploads/2017/07/A-Role-of-the-Private-Sector-in-21st Century-Global-Migration-Policy.pdf

Grierson, J. (2018, August 27). Hostile environment: Anatomy of a policy disaster. *The Guardian* Retrieved from http://www.theguardian.com/uk-news/2018/aug/27/hostile-environment-anatomy-of-a-policy-disaster

Haslam, N., & Stratemeyer, M. (2016). Recent research on dehumanization. *Current Opinion in Psychology*, *11*, 25–29.

Heath, A. F., & Tilley, J. R. (2005). British national identity and attitudes towards immigration. *International Journal on Multicultural Societies*, *7*(2), 119–132.

Home Office. (2014a, May). Code of practice for employers: Avoiding unlawful discrimination while preventing illegal working. Retrieved from https://assets.publishing.service.gov.uk/government/uploads/system/uploads/attachment_data/file/311665/Code_of_practice_on_avoiding_unlawful_discrimination_while_preventing_illegal_working.pdf

Home Office. (2014b, July 28). An employer's guide to the Administration of the Civil Penalty Scheme. Retrieved from https://assets.publishing.service.gov.uk/government/uploads/system/uploads/attachment_data/file/338061/civil_penalty_scheme_-_28_July_2014.pdf

Home Office. (2019a, January). Code of practice on preventing illegal working: Civil Penalty Scheme for employers. Retrieved from https://assets.publishing.service.gov.uk/government/uploads/system/uploads/attachment_data/file/774078/Code_of_practice_on_preventing_illegal_working_-_January_2019.pdf

Home Office. (2019b, January 28). An employer's guide to right to work checks. Retrieved from https://assets.publishing.service.gov.uk/government/uploads/system/uploads/attachment_data/file/773780/An_employer_s_guide_to_right_to_work_checks_-_January_2019.pdf

Hough, A. (2012, November 6). Tesco fined £115,000 for employing illegal foreign workers. *The Telegraph.* Retrieved from http://www.telegraph.co.uk/news/uknews/immigration/9658297/Tesco-fined-115000-for-employing-illegal-foreign-workers.html

House of Commons Home Affairs Committee. (2018, January 15). Immigration Policy: Basis for building consensus. Retrieved from https://publications.parliament.uk/pa/cm201719/cmselect/cmhaff/500/500.pdf

The Joint Council for the Welfare of Immigrants. (2015, September 3). 'No passport equals no home': An independent evaluation of the Right to Rent Scheme. Retrieved from https://www.jcwi.org.uk/Handlers/Download.ashx?IDMF=5ab15f33-ae32-4e66-b040-402b71392177

Khosravi, S. (2007). The 'Illegal' traveller: An auto-ethnography of borders. *Social Anthropology/Anthropologie Sociale*, *15*(3), 321–334.

Levitas, R., Pantazis, C., Fahmy, E., Gordon, D., Lloyd, E., & Patsios, D. (2007). The multi-dimensional analysis of social exclusion. Retrieved from https://www.researchgate.net/publication/267222796_The_Multi-Dimensional_Analysis_of_Social_Exclusion

Mack, J. (2016, January 21). Social exclusion. Retrieved from http://www.poverty.ac.uk/definitions-poverty/social-exclusion

Massey, D. S., & Gentsch, K. (2014). Un-documented migration to the United States and the wages of Mexican immigrants. *International Migration Review*, *48*(2), 482–499.

McKay, S., & Wright, T. (2008). Tightening immigration policies and labour market impacts. *Transfer: European Review of Labour and Research*, *14*(4), 653–664.

Morris, S. (2018, January 2). Trio who used trafficked girls to work in nail bars jailed under slavery laws. *The Guardian*. Retrieved from https://www.theguardian.com/world/2018/jan/02/trio-trafficked-girls-work-nail-bars-jailed-slavery-laws-uk

Nessel, L. A. (2015). Deliberate destitution as deterrent: Withholding the right to work and undermining asylum protection. *San Diego Law Review*, *52*, 313–356.

Nyberg Sørensen, N. (2012). Revisiting the migration–development nexus: From social networks and remittances to markets for migration control. *International Migration*, *50*(3), 61–76.

Poole, S. (2018, May 3). Compliant environment: Is this really what the Windrush Generation needs? *The Guardian*. Retrieved from http://www.theguardian.com/books/2018/may/03/compliant-environment-is-this-really-what-the-windrush-generation-needs

Ryan, B. (2005). The evolving Legal Regime on unauthorized work by migrants in Britain. *Comparative Labor Law and Policy Journal*, *27*, 27–58.

Ryan, B. (2014). Employer checks of immigration status and employment law. In C. Costello & M. Freedland (Eds.), *Migrants at work: Immigration and vulnerability in labour law* (pp. 239–257). Oxford: Oxford University Press.

Smith, A. D. (1972). Ethnocentrism, nationalism and social change. *International Journal of Comparative Sociology*, *13*(1), 1–20.

Steele, S. E. (2008). Deterrence to hiring illegal immigrant workers: Will the new employer sanction provisions work. *Georgia Journal of International and Comparative Law*, *36*, 475–509.

Suarez Congdon, R. (2008). Comparing employer sanctions provisions and employment eligibility verification procedures in the United States and the United Kingdom. *Indiana International and Comparative Law Review*, *18*(2), 391–435.

Tendayi Achiume, E. (2018, May 11). End of Mission Statement of the Special Rapporteur on contemporary forms of racism, racial discrimination, xenophobia and related intolerance at the conclusion of Her Mission to the United Kingdom of Great Britain and Northern Ireland. Retrieved from https://www.ohchr.org/EN/NewsEvents/Pages/DisplayNews.aspx?NewsID=23073&LangID=E

Utych, S. M. (2018). How dehumanization influences attitudes toward immigrants. *Political Research Quarterly*, *71*(2), 440–452.

Valentine, R. (2010). Hope costs nothing: The lives of undocumented migrants in the UK. Retrieved from https://www.migrantsresourcecentre.org.uk/wp-content/uploads/2013/06/Hope-costs-nothing.pdf

Victor, P. (1995, October 5). Cabinet rift on jobs 'Racism'. *The Independent.* Retrieved from http://www.independent.co.uk/news/cabinet-rift-on-jobs-racism-1575985.html

Walsh, J. P. (2014). Watchful citizens: Immigration control, surveillance and societal participation. *Social and Legal Studies*, *23*(2), 237–259.

Zembylas, M. (2010). Agamben's Theory of biopower and immigrants/refugees/asylum seekers. *Journal of Curriculum Theorizing*, *26*(2), 31–45.

CHAPTER 4

IN THE CONTEXT OF THE AGRICULTURAL INDUSTRY, TO WHAT EXTENT DOES THE UK GOVERNMENT'S 'HOSTILE ENVIRONMENT' AGENDA OUTWEIGH THE IMPACT OF THE MODERN SLAVERY ACT 2015 ON IRREGULAR WORKERS?

Harriet Parfitt

ABSTRACT

The 'hostile environment' agenda of Government has effectively endorsed the deliberate exploitation of irregular migrants in the agricultural industry. This minor project of jurisprudence will provide two arguments in support of this hypothesis. Firstly, the vulnerabilities faced by irregular migrants are reinforced through the xenophobic narrative embodied within the law and the courts. The lack of priority afforded to modern slavery on the UK Policy Agenda has allowed a 'grey labour market' (1) to develop. Irregular migrants face a 'precarity paradox' and (2) they must avoid the carceral regime of immigration control by entering into unprotected and deliberately exploitative work. Secondly, a lacklustre attempt to remedy the corruption

Privatisation of Migration Control: Power without Accountability?
Studies in Law, Politics, and Society, Volume 86B, 57–73

ISSN: 1059-4337/doi:10.1108/S1059-433720210000086B005

in the horticultural industry proves that the state is preoccupied, capitalising on irregular labour practice in the interests of state capital. Thus, the Government allows the commodification of workers within the supply chain to profit British businesses.

Keywords: Modern Slavery; irregular labour; precarious; exploitation; agriculture; commodification

The Internal Monologue of an Irregular Migrant Labourer

My bones are broken

My stomach: empty

My hands are dirty

My scars a plenty

My rights – what rights?

No justice prevails in this nation

For it is I who sought this illegal existence

Albeit it to escape deportation

They did a license check last night

A random; unplanned 'hello'

I was hidden – the inspectors missed me

My *Master* reassured me so

Wages paid tomorrow!

Last month's pittance has already been spent

10p envelope, 20p stamp

So back home this money can be sent

It's a temporary fix, I reassure myself

As I sleep amongst the rats

In denial that I cannot escape

The grasp of the aristocrats

INTRODUCTION

The protection afforded to victims of deliberate exploitation in the agricultural industry is significantly caveated by the state's alternative investment in protecting British borders and business. This academic inquiry is premised on two concerns that arise from announcement of the post-Brexit Seasonal Workers Pilot scheme (SWP). This migration programme will offer only 2,500 visas to migrants seeking work in horticulture (The Home Office and the Department for Food and Rural Affairs; see also Secretary of State for the Home Department, 2018), restricting the number of employment opportunities in agriculture on the UK labour market for non-UK citizens. Thus, migrants seeking work in this sector will be forced to enter illegal regimes of labour provision in the absence of a visa, establishing environments for deliberate exploitation. Simultaneously, private labour providers will operate increasingly outside the remit of the law, in an attempt to evade carceral punishment for the offence of illegal work practice.[1] This will inhibit the efforts of the state to abolish gangmasters; large-scale employers who perpetuate the practice of modern slavery.

The policy shift from an 'employment … to an immigration control agenda' (Davies, 2014, p. 1) in the agricultural industry now requires further investigation, in light of significant legislative developments since Davies' initial exploration of this niche in 2014. Section I of this chapter will rationalise this transition by assessing the impact of two watershed statutes, the Modern Slavery Act 2015 (MSA 2015) and the Immigration Act 2016 (IA 2016), on the UK policy agenda. Corresponding, the judiciary has played an undeniable role in furthering the incoherence of the law on modern slavery, which Section II of this chapter will demonstrate. In order to come to a conclusion over which Act the state is most invested in Section III of this chapter will critically evaluate the scholarly consensus that 'concerns of immigration control trump concerns of labour exploitation' (Mantouvalou, 2018, pp. 1017–1036). This project will prove how the political incentive to maximise state capital, coupled with the sentiments of the 'hostile environment' policy, has an overwhelming influence on the sub-standard regulation of illegal work. To strengthen this argument, Section VI will utilise the lens of Marxism to clarify how the state capitalises on the commodification of irregular migrants.

The legal manifestations of nationalism 'in the political form of xenophobia' (Attas, 2000), and the 'dominant neoliberal discourse' (Attas, 2000) in the labour market, undeniably caveat the state campaign against deliberate exploitation. This discussion will provide a balanced account of whether the impact of these alternative agendas of the state goes beyond reasonable justification.

SECTION I: A CONFLICT OF INTEREST – THE LEGAL PARADOX

Modern Slavery: A Revived Crusade

The European Court of Human Rights (ECtHR) only gradually recognised modern slavery as an international pandemic. A series of cases highlighted the pressing need to address labour exploitation by making the severity of its consequences apparent. Access to Article 4 of the European Convention on Human Rights (ECHR) was considered jeopardised under the legislative framework of multiple jurisdictions.

1. No one shall be held in slavery or servitude.
2. No one shall be required to perform forced or compulsory labour.[2]

Modern slavery is a 'portmanteau term' (Fudge, 2018a, pp. 414–415), because it encompasses multiple archetypes of unjust treatment of irregular migrants in illegal labour relationships. The term 'labour' will be applied throughout this discussion, as most illegal work is not founded upon contract and therefore falls out of the scope of 'employment'. Accordingly, 'workers' and 'labour providers' will replace the commonplace 'employer' and 'employee' dichotomy. The definitions of these four categories of deliberate exploitation have been expanded upon in common law. In *Siliadan*, the court ruled that slavery ought to be interpreted in conjunction with 'ownership', under Section 1(1) of the 1926 UN Slavery Convention.[3] This must be distinguished from the concept of servitude, which is defined in *Van Droogenbroeck*, as a 'particularly serious form of denial of freedom'.[4] Finally, the concept of forced and compulsory labour was synchronously interpreted in *Van der Mussele* as service exacted from an individual 'under the menace of any penalty'[5]; it is severable from 'servitude' because it necessitates the feeling of inescapability.[6] In the variety of instances of deliberate exploitation in contemporary agriculture, it is practical to address these terms collectively as 'modern slavery'. As a final point of clarification, the term 'deliberate exploitation' (Carens, 2008, p. 432) refers to the consequences of modern slavery. This formulation by Carel is distinct from 'exploitation', which can be judged subjectively in the wider employment sphere. Thus, it is designed 'to avoid prejudging the debate about the moral legitimacy of normal market transactions' (Carens, 2008, pp. 419–432), and helps to confine the discussion to the certified irregular operation of agricultural labour.

Undeniably, the protective measures against modern slavery offered by the UK do not exist in a domestic vacuum. As evidenced in the aforementioned discussion of *Siliadan*, it is commonplace for the ECtHR to refer to international treaty obligations when interpreting Article 4. To name but a few constitutional instruments that the Court has relied on: the Supplementary Convention on the Abolition of Slavery was incorporated in *CN and V v. France*,[7] the International Labour Organisation (ILO) Convention No. 29 (Forced Labour Convention) in *Van der Mussele*,[8] and Council of Europe Convention on Action against Trafficking in Human Beings in *Rantsev*.[9] This chapter, by virtue of its limited scope, is unable to do justice to the significant body of legislation in this field. This discussion will be confined to the effectiveness of national legislation in aiding the contemporary campaign against deliberate exploitation in the agricultural sector, despite the potential influence of these legal apparatuses on the simultaneous intercontinental movement.

The state has made an undeniable effort to fulfil both the obligation to protect potential or confirmed victims of modern slavery, identified in *Silidan*,[10] and the duty to investigate and penalise instances of trafficking, where individuals are transported for the purposes of deliberately exploitative labour regimes, established in *Rantsev*.[11] As a signatory to the ECHR, the UK legislature must incorporate this case law into its internal framework, and the UK courts ought to interpret subsequent law to comply with it, so far as it is possible to do so.[12]

These intentions were manifested in the criminalisation of modern slavery under Section 71 of the Coroners and Justice Act 2009.[13] This was quickly succeeded by the 'historic milestone' (The Home Office, Bradley & May, 2015) of the MSA 2015 after the jurisdiction of the UK fell under the scrutiny of the ECtHR in *CN v. UK*.[14] Crucially, this expanded the powers of the Gangmasters Licensing Authority (GLAA), previously established under the Gangmasters Licensing Act 2004 (GLA 2004),[15] whose prerogative over the regulation of the private provision of labour increased.

Nonetheless, the impetus of this academic inquiry is founded upon the contrasting sentiments expressed in the subsequent IA 2016, which crystallised the 'hostile environment' towards irregular workers. The Act promoted a 'hateful policy agenda' (The hostile environment for immigrants: How Theresa May has created an underclass in the UK, 2018) against illegal migrants, which can be interpreted as a legislative caveat to the MSA 2015. Although the Government pledged that the Act was designed to 'protect'[16] and not to punish the vulnerable, in reality 'the picture has been bleaker since' (Byrne, 2018) for these individuals. This claim will be substantiated throughout the entirety of this chapter. When mapped against the proclamation that modern slavery is 'the greatest human rights issue of our time' (May, 2016), these dichotomous narratives of protection and prosecution embody the 'paradox of precarity'[17] that the convoluted UK Policy Agenda has created for private labour relationships involving irregular migrants. It leaves undocumented workers with a choice between a rock and a hard place: 'destitution or exploitative employment in the shadow economy'.[18] These are shaky foundations for irregular workers approaching a post-Brexit era.

Immigration Control: An Overriding Interest

In the current political climate, governed by a nationalist interest to protect the integrity of the state and its capital during Brexit, it is unlikely that an equitable balance can be struck between these two contradictory regimes. The shift in state priorities from 'employment … to … immigration control'[19] was crystallised in 2014, when control of the GLAA, formerly under the remit of the Department for Food and Rural Affairs, was reallocated to the jurisdiction of the Home Office (Gangmasters Licensing Authority and Others, 2014). The implication of this is paramount: modern slavery is no longer viewed as an isolated pandemic as the allocation of resources towards this cause must now be weighed against the contrasting state interest in curbing immigration. Thus, unsurprisingly, between 2014 and 2016, only 384 of 2,563 victims of modern slavery were granted discretionary leave to remain in the UK (Burland, 2017). The suggestion of an automatic right to remain was dismissed as a 'pull factor'[20] that would encourage fraudulent individuals to abuse the system of immigration control. The deportation of these victims directly contravenes May's promise that the IA 2016 would not punish the vulnerable.

This macrostructural change in policy had a devastating effect on microinstances of deliberate exploitation in labour relationships, agricultural or otherwise. A firewall, a term used to describe the separation of immigration enforcement and labour inspection, is renowned as 'a key mechanism for labour inspectorates to do their jobs well' (Ishibashi, 2019). However, in her critique of the IA 2016, Robinson exposes a significant interpersonal ramification of the Home Office's prerogative over the two dichotomous agendas. She argues that the lack of firewall has severed the 'all-important trust' (Robinson, 2015) between labour inspectorates and victims of deliberate exploitation. Gangmasters, confident that migrants will continue to work within their unscrupulous labour regime rather than jeopardise their UK residence, offer these vulnerable individuals a non-contractual exchange. By illegally negating their 'right to work'[21] checks, gangmasters can systematically exploit these irregular workers with impunity. Notably, these consequences of privatisation are not limited to labour relations – the IA 2014 permitted landlords to request immigration documentation, with residential tenancy agreements granted almost exclusively to 'relevant nationals'.[22] This additional consideration only provides further clarification as to why the Independent Anti-Slavery Commissioner, Kevin Hyland, resigned in May 2018. The words of his resignation embodied the reality that the capacity for Government to combat deliberate exploitation is, more often than not, 'discretionary from the Home Office, rather than legally bestowed' (Hyland, 2018).

Section I exemplified the complex interplay between the agendas of the MSA 2015 and IA 2016. Against this legal backdrop, the remainder of this chapter will demonstrate the effect that these two contesting projects – one, a liberal crusade against the deliberate exploitation of private workers, and the other, a hostile crackdown on immigration by private labour providers – has had on the rights and societal perception of irregular migrant agricultural workers in the public sphere.

SECTION II: EXPLOITATION IN AGRICULTURE – A PRODUCT OF NATURE OR NURTURE?

Agriculture: A Flawed Industry

The ILO has cautioned that temporary migration programmes, such as the SWP, should not enable 'the curtailment of the rights of migrant workers' (International Labour Office, 2006). Despite this, there is a sufficient evidential basis to argue that agribusiness presents a high-risk environment for labour exploitation (Phillips & Trautrims, 2018), irrespective of irregularity on the part of the migrant, the labour provider or the state. This argument is founded on empirical data collected in the aftermath of the Seasonal Agricultural Workers Visa programme (SAWS). This transnational agreement, which permitted UK entry to nationals of Bulgaria and Romania whose EU membership was yet to actualise, was far from evading accountability for instances of deliberate exploitation (Kenway, 2018).

The hypersensitivity of the sector is evidenced by the compatibility of the practices of the agricultural industry with Paz-Fuch's (2016) 'badges of slavery' (p. 757), which embody characteristics archetypal of contemporary instances of deliberate exploitation. This analysis was undertaken using two significant badges 'uniquely applicable' (Paz-Fuchs, 2016, p. 764) to labour relationships, which are starkly apropos to the jobs delegated to irregular migrants in modern agriculture. The first of these badges is 'sub-standard terms and conditions of the employment' (Paz-Fuchs, 2016, p. 779), which, by reason of their extremity and derogatory nature, often 'shatter an individual's dignity' (Paz-Fuchs, 2016, p. 779). Agricultural work is heavily laborious, especially in the peak season when migrants under the SWP will be relied upon. This provides an apt explanation as to why this work is pioneered by migrants; their 'submissive malleability' (Surak, 2013, pp. 84–86) makes these individuals preferable to British workers. Their willingness to undertake 'the undignified tasks that natives shun' (Surak, 2013, p. 86) normalises non-UK citizens as the 'backbone'[23] of the industry. Secondly, the venues of agricultural work are often geographically isolated, by virtue of the natural distribution of horticultural land mass suitable for cultivation. Commonplace farming practice all but forces workers to eat and sleep on the land they harvest. This means that with little knowledge of the local area, and the inability to accumulate income to travel, any alternative labour opportunities remain unexplored and inaccessible. This setting warrants an application of Paz-Fuch's second badge, 'limits on the power to end the employment relationship'.[24] These burdens of the agricultural industry mean that the vulnerability of workers working without a valid immigration status will only be 'enhanced' (Rogaly, 2008, pp. 497–501).

Remedial Action: The Inconsistency of the Courts

The agricultural industry is a causal factor in the continuation of deliberate exploitation, so the courts must pre-empt and react swiftly to instances of injustice. An active judicial effort to deliver suitable remedial action would sufficiently reduce the impact of modern slavery. More significantly, an obligation on the state to redress instances of violation of freedom is imposed under Article 13 of the ECHR.[25] It is unclear whether the initial narrative of protection effectuated under the MSA 2015 holds enough weight to trump the long-standing judicial crusade to uphold the doctrine of illegality: 'no court will lend its aid to a man who founds his cause of action upon an immoral or illegal act'.[26] This assessment must be made in light of the criminalisation of illegal work under Section 34 of the IA 2016.[27] Despite the fact that cases in the context of agricultural labour would initially be brought in employment tribunals, a holistic consideration of the court system in its entirety will prove the overarching consequence of the common law principle on commonplace judicial ethos.

The Agricultural Wages Board (AWB) addressed the heightened precarity in agricultural labour by mandating modified pay grades for its workers, which accounted for the onerous burdens of the industry (Agricultural Workers Rights). Its positive impact was evidenced in *Galdikas v. Houghton*, where Supperstone J awarded damages to seven Lithuanian trafficking victims whose gangmasters had failed to meet these requirements.[28] However, the claimants were protected under the AWB only by virtue of their work on the poultry farm prior to 2013 – the year the AWB was scrapped by the Government to curb public spending.[29] This governmental prioritisation of protecting state capital over the rights of migrant workers is an established pattern in UK policy, which will be addressed in Section III of this chapter. More importantly, there is now no definitive mechanism to hold irregular labour providers civilly liable for unpaid wages.

The judiciary have instead legitimised an 'indeterminate' (Fudge, 2018b) framework, where the dichotomous policy concerns of preventing modern slavery and condemning illegal work alternatively take centre stage. The judiciary initially upheld their campaign against modern slavery to the extent that it was deemed a sufficient reason to countervail the aforementioned maxim of contract law: an action does not arise from a dishonourable cause (ex turpi causa non oritur action). Whilst a claim to tort right is barred when 'inextricably linked' with an illegal action, such a claim was successful in the context of racial discrimination in *Hounga*.[30] Similarly, a restitutionary remedy was permitted in Patel by virtue of the facts,[31] despite the general rule that unjust enrichment claims are barred by illegality.[32] In both instances, the Supreme Court deemed that endorsing a claim under the operation of an illegal contract within the wider interest of protecting the vulnerable would not compromise the integrity of the legal system. The judiciary had 'mitigated the harshness of the illegality doctrine on social rights of irregular migrants' (Bogg & Green, 2015, p. 101).

Nonetheless, the courts have since retracted this concession made to irregular workers. It is arguable that Lord Hughes' dicta in *Hounga*; that the law must not 'condone when facing right what it condemns when facing left',[33] and Lord Toulson's synonymous statement in *Patel*; 'the law should be ... not self-defeating',[34] only foreshadowed a self-fulfilling prophecy. The Court of Appeal confined *Patel* to cases of unjust enrichment and contract in a recent tort case of *Henderson v. Dorset Healthcare*.[35] This is of particular concern in the context of deliberate exploitation, as the right to non-discrimination is a tort right under the 'compartmentalised' (Bogg, 2018, forthcoming, p. 3) stratification of rights in employment tribunals. The court system has created a platform which enables labour providers, who deliberately disadvantage their irregular workers, to evade accountability by virtue of the very illegality upon which their regime is founded upon. This unqualified protection of social rights has substantively 'constitutionalised' (Bogg, 2018, forthcoming, p. 2) the 'paradox of precarity'.[36] Byrne's supporting observation, that 'a hostile environment for undocumented migrants is a hospitable environment for modern slave drivers',[37] contributes a significant degree of weight to this argument. The incoherence of state rhetoric, governed by the multifaceted agenda of the Home Office, serves to benefit only those in the position to capitalise upon it.

The 'institutionalised uncertainty' (Anderson, 2010, pp. 300–301) promulgated by the judiciary, who have failed to provide steadfast protection to irregular migrants facing injustice within the agricultural industry, is more than sufficient proof that the state has taken advantage of the non-codified nature of the right to a sufficient remedy under Article 13 of the ECHR.[38] This could bring the UK's legislative framework back under the scrutiny of the ECtHR, as it is dubious whether the ECHR has been incorporated so far as it is possible to do so, or at the very should least warrant a review by the Law Commission of the rights of irregular migrants in the tribunal system. Parliament is permitted, as sovereign, to legislate contrary to fundamental human rights if it can 'accept the political cost'.[39] Despite Lord Hoffman's apparent restraint on this prerogative in *ex parte Simms*, the 'political' ramifications will remain a burden carried by undocumented workers. The 'cost' of their labour, however, seems all too willingly 'accepted' by the state, a controversy that the second half of this project will now expand upon.

SECTION III: A HIDDEN AGENDA – THE 'SMOKE AND MIRRORS'[40] OF CAPITALISM

Licensing Law: Ulterior Motives

The GLAA, as the independent regulator of the agricultural sector,[41] is responsible for ensuring that labour providers 'operate within the law' (Gangmaster and Labour Abuse Authority). The operation of the GLAA has undeniably reduced the capacity for deliberately exploitative slavery practice in contemporary agricultural labour. This is evidenced by the reduction of unlicensed labour providers in the UK market. Under the GLA 2004, gangmasters can only legally operate with a license.[42] If they breach the conditions under which the license was granted, it can be revoked.[43] In 2008, out of all the gangmasters who were deemed unfit for a license by virtue of their improper working practices, less than 12 per cent had outstanding conditions to fulfil by the end of the year (Bance & Poinasamy, 2009). Prima facie, this seems an effective operational measure to protect potential or confirmed victims of modern slavery, as required of the state by *Rantsev*.[44] More labour practices ought to now meet the requisite standard deemed appropriate for workers, and improper labour practices in the agricultural industry should be on the decline.

However, further investigation into the genesis of the GLA 2004 proves that the campaign against modern slavery may not have motivated the substantive reform. The Private Member's Bill which prompted the enactment of the legislation came to the attention of Parliament only as a result of the death of 23 Chinese migrant workers at Morecambe Bay. This infamous tragedy is personified in Broomfield's *Ghosts* (2006), which depicts how the protagonist Al Qin, a Chinese cockle-picker, was failed by her gangmaster, who allowed his workers to drown at high tide.[45] Rogaly describes the Act's advocates as 'an unlikely grouping',[46] referring to the large number of retailers who partook in the legislative campaign. It can therefore be argued that the GLA 2004 was premised on the protection of British business from bad publicity. The involvement of the media through the production of *Ghosts* proves the societal urge to expose this controversy. The 79 per cent of gangmasters in favour of the licensing were not invested in the rights of irregular migrants.[47] Instead, they wished for a restoration of consumer faith in the ethical code of supermarkets, to whom they supplied their horticultural products. Fudge's proclamation that the state will only make a 'business case and not a human ... rights case'[48] for enforcing labour standards prompts the additional evaluation that the politics of the supply chain was not the only hidden agenda behind the enactment of the GLA 2004. The Act is now self-perpetuating – licensed gangmasters are incentivised to report illegal gangmasters, who capitalise on deliberate exploitation to undercut competitors who guarantee their workers basic legal rights. This positive feedback loop serves to relieve the GLAA of the burden to investigate. The resources of the Home Office can instead be concentrated upon the 'hostile environment' agenda.

Supply Chains: A 'State–Business Nexus'[49]

The state is just as culpable as the businesses that operate within the parameters of its neoliberal market. It manipulates the GLA 2004 into a politico-economic axe to grind for the interests of profit. This argument is formulated on an attestation by Brass (2004), that 'the role of the gangmaster is a systemic one, reproduced by capitalism itself' (pp. 313–321). The role of the gangmaster is 'systemic' because it is governed by the horticultural supply chain. This system entails a 'concentration of power amongst a relatively small number of transnational food producers and retailers' (Geddes & Scott, 2010, p. 1), underneath which are increasingly smaller-sized enterprises. Between companies offering the same labour, competition to obtain a profitable sub-contract rises. Mantouvalou claimed that the issue of supply chain regulation is not 'directly linked'[50] to immigration, but this chapter contends this argument, and will consider her statement in the alternative. Geddes motivates this reverse enquiry, professing that an influx of irregular migrant workers 'eager for employment'[51] increases productivity and cuts labour costs. Their uptake of low-paid work is the 'easiest response to falling profit margins',[52] which is why exploitative gangmasters supply some of the UK's major supermarkets. The effectiveness of combating worker exploitation is thus 'inextricably linked'[53] to the purchasing practices of the supermarkets. In times of austerity, the state must adhere to the 'political imperative' (Strauss, 2013, p. 180) to keep food prices low. Thus, it is undeniable that the state's fiscal agenda severely contradicts its efforts to eradicate modern slavery.

This alternative agenda of the state rationalises the lack of enforceability of the MSA 2015, premised on addressing the negative repercussions of the trend of supply and demand. Martin-Ortega argued that the 'Transparency in Supply Chains' provision of the MSA 2015 has proved a 'catalyst for a wider process of understanding the human rights risks attached to institution's commercial relations'.[54] This claim cannot be sufficiently substantiated in the context of the agricultural industry. Although Section 54 requires businesses to publish an annual report on the composition of their supply chain,[55] it does not mandate the statement's contents, nor does it require any action beyond its publication. A lack of sanction for non-compliance has meant the law is adhered by a narrow majority: only 56 per cent of FTSE 100 companies complied with Section 54 (Business and Human Rights Resource Centre, 2017). Moreover, the state has afforded little attention to alternative mechanisms to expose exploitation within commercial supply chains. One example is ethical auditing, where the lower tiers of production are scrutinised at regular intervals per annum (LeBaron & Rühmkorf, 2017). This would benefit seasonal migrants, who, due to temporary nature of their work, may fall outside the remit of the infrequent bouts of auditing in the current system.

The Modern Slavery (Transparency in Supply Chains) Bill sought to include public bodies in the transparency requirements of the MSA.[56] The Home Office, as a public body, could be liable for supplying SWP participants to deliberately exploitative labour. This accountability would motivate greater regulation of the supply chain, and thus, provide a benefit for irregular workers from private labour relationships too. Nonetheless, this Bill was scrapped following the dissolution of Parliament in June 2017. This was motivated by a political need for a snap election to reformulate a majority in support of Brexit. It seems a recurrent theme that 'accountability norms ... [are] trumped by the power of economic interests',[57] exemplified by both large corporations and state actors. The Government has addressed alternative social concerns in the food industry, including 'the decline of small independent shops ... [and] the environmental impacts of out of town shopping'.[58] These efforts act as 'smoke and mirrors'[59] to distract those unaffected by the unresolved issue of the vulnerabilities of the agricultural sector. A final paradox arises from this constitutional choice: 'the price we pay for cheap food is a very high one indeed'.[60] Section VI of this project will expand upon the societal implications of this oxymoronic state of affairs.

SECTION IV: CRYSTALLISING THE POWER IMBALANCE – A SOCIO-LEGAL PERSPECTIVE

The Hegemonic State

The neglect of modern slavery from the policy agenda proves doubly advantageous for the state: not only does it profit the UK food industry, but it enables latent xenophobia embedded in the status quo to prevail unchallenged. This argument is based on the theory of social reproduction. Marx (1990) hypothesised that wages are socially determined, as a result of the dependence of the reproductive cycle of society on the political economy. This structure 'transmit[s] social inequality from one generation to the next' (Doob, 2003); hence, when applied to the context of agricultural labour, it exemplifies how the state continues to profit from deliberate exploitation. The inherent state interest in the accumulation of capital has only catalysed the institutionalisation of a 'tradeoff between rights and numbers',[61] originally promulgated by the governmental priority afforded to immigration control over modern slavery victims. The claim by Fudge, that 'the figure of the migrant has been ... harnessed to ... an internal governance project ... to tame the "free" market with ... political norms',[62] alludes to how the patterns of modern slavery in society warrant continuity and little change. On the basis that state reform is governed by the self-interest, Gramscian theory explains how this 'internal government project' is sustained, identifying that 'for a class or social group to attain a dominant position in a given society, it had [to] ... act in the interests of the vulnerable'.[63] By the state's apparent effort to target modern slavery through the GLAA, 'the British hegemony and its adherence to the utopian free market creed'[64] prevails. Likewise, the MSA 2015 only crystalised the 'political norm' of xenophobia in doing little to challenge this discourse, by virtue of its many caveats.

'The Alien Other'[65]

At the other end of the power spectrum, the normalisation of precarious undocumented labour has constitutionalised the societal subordination of irregular migrants. When viewed through a Marxist lens, these individuals personify the defining feature of capitalist labour relations: exploitation through improper wage payment to generate a surplus value which accrues to capital. The 'revolving door style recruitment'[66] in irregular labour, evidenced by the impartiality of gangmasters to the deportation of their workers by the Home Office, is akin to Marx's notion of the non-identity in agriculture.[67] This reduces these individuals to cogs in the 'machine': a 'means for producing surplus-value'.[68] This is why irregular migration is a system of labour supply 'particularly suited' (Sassen, 1988, p. 40) to deliberately exploitative practices. Through applying the theory of social reproduction to irregular agricultural labour, the ILO's affirmation that 'people, unlike commodities, are conscious actors' (Chammartin & Taran, 2003) is embedded with irony. Migrants consciously determine their own commodification.

Mantouvalou (2015) concurs that irregular migrant labourers in the agricultural sector are 'not only in a position of subordination typical of the employment relation' but 'in a state of true objectification'. This is because the 'discourses of the alien Other'[69] are promulgated by the state and migrants simultaneously. Undocumented workers, faced with a 'paradox of precarity',[70] undertake deliberately exploitative labour, manifesting the role of both actor and victim in the determination of their fate. Their willingness to work these 'dirty, degrading and dangerous' '3d jobs' (International Labour Conference, 2004) lead to 'the commodification of European mobile work' (Van Ostaijen, Reeger, & Zelano, 2017, pp. 1–2), or in Rogaly's words, a 'commodity fetishism'[71] on behalf of British businesses. In retrospect, the 'historic milestone' promised by the MSA 2015 has been far from delivered: the associations of gang labour with 'Dickensian overtones'[72] confirms the agricultural industry as a relic of 'Thomas Hardy's England'.[73] This degree of continuity, with victims of deliberate exploitation coined as the 'new Victorian servant class' (Favell, 2008, pp. 701–711), is far from justifiable in twenty-first century Britain.

CONCLUSION

Irregular migrants in agricultural labour are deliberately exploited. This pandemic is not only poorly regulated by the Government, but also capitalised upon by state actors, proving modern slavery not only to be outweighed on the UK policy agenda, but eradicated from it almost entirely. This is somewhat accounted for by the hegemonic state influence over the 'Other', endorsed through the xenophobic ideologies that motivate law and society. These discourses pervade the labour market in so far as to ensure that irregular migrant workers are objectified, but worse still, tolerate their own commodification. However, the clear priority of the state to maximise the profitability of British businesses manifests a greater caveat to the MSA 2015 agenda than the 'hostile environment' measures of the IA 2016. A Marxist analysis proves this is an archetypal consequence of the capitalist framework of a neoliberal state, where the economy governs society in the place of policy. In a post-Brexit climate, this controversy will only be aggravated by the limited provision of SWPs. There will be fewer labour opportunities operating within the parameters of legality, and irregular migrants will be obliged to reinforce state interests by seeking irregular work.

NOTES

1. Immigration Act 2016, s. 34.
2. European Convention on Human Rights, art 4.
3. *Siliadin v. France* App no 73316/01 (ECHR, 26 July 2005) [122].
4. *Van Droogenbroeck* v. *Belgium* (Commission's Report, 9 July 1980) [78–80].
5. *Van der Mussele v. Belgium* (1984) 6 EHRR 163 [32].
6. *Chowdury and Others v. Greece* App no 21884/15 (ECHR, 30 March 2017) [99].
7. *CN and V v. France* App no 67724/09 (ECHR, 11 October 2012) [90].
8. *Van der Mussele* (n 13) [32].
9. *Rantsev v. Cyprus and Russia* App no 25965/04 (ECHR, 7 January 2010) [282].
10. *Siliadin* (n 11) [149].
11. *Rantsev* (n 19) [285].
12. Human Rights Act 1998, s. 3.
13. Coroners and Justice Act 2009, s. 71.
14. *CN v. UK* App no 4239/08 (ECHR, 13 November 2012) [94].
15. Modern Slavery Act 2015, s. 13.
16. HC Deb 1 December 2015, vol 603, cols 175–181.
17. Freedland, 'The Contract of Employment' (n 2) 1.
18. Byrne (n 29).
19. Davies (n 5) 1.
20. Work and Pensions Committee, *Victims of Modern Slavery* (HC 2016-2017, 803-XII).
21. Immigration Act 2016, s. 34.
22. Immigration Act 2014, s. 21(1)(a).
23. Strauss, 'Challenging Hegemonic Deregulation?' (n 1) 1.
24. Paz-Fuchs (n 45) 783.
25. ECHR (n 9) art 13.
26. *Holman v. Johnson* (1775) 1 Cowp 341 [343] (Lord Mansfield CJ).
27. Immigration Act 2016, s. 34.
28. *Galdikas v. Houghton* [2016] EWHC 1376 (QB) [25] (Supperstone J).
29. Enterprise and Regulatory Reform Act 2013, s. 72.
30. *Hounga v. Allen* [2014] UKSC 47.
31. *Patel v. Mirza* [2016] UKSC 42.
32. *Tinsley v. Milligan* [1993] UKHL 3.
33. *Hounga* (n 61) [55] (Lord Hughes).
34. *Patel* (n 62) [99] (Lord Toulson).
35. *Henderson v. Dorset Healthcare* [2018] EWCA Civ 1841.
36. Freedland, 'The Contract of Employment' (n 2) 1.
37. Byrne (n 29).
38. ECHR (n 9) art 4.
39. *R* v. *Secretary of State for the Home Department ex parte Simms* [1999] UKHL 33 [131] (Lord Hoffman).
40. Anderson (2015, p. 69).
41. Gangmasters Licensing Act 2004, s. (3)(1)(a).
42. Gangmasters Licensing Act 2004, s. 6(1).
43. Gangmasters Licensing Act 2004, s. 9(1)(b).
44. *Rantsev* (n 19) [286].
45. Nick Broomfield, *Ghosts* (2006).
46. Rogaly (n 53) 502.
47. Bance and Poinasamy (n 80) 12.
48. Fudge, 'Illegal Working' (n 60) 581.
49. Martin-Ortega (2017, pp. 512–513).
50. Mantouvalou, 'The UK Modern Slavery Act' (n 6) 1037.
51. Geddes and Scott (n 88) 1.
52. Geddes and Scott (n 88) 1.
53. Bance and Poinasamy (n 80) 18.

54. Martin-Ortega (n 86) 512.
55. Modern Slavery Act, s. 54.
56. Modern Slavery (Transparency in Supply Chains) Bill [HL] (2016–17) 105.
57. LeBaron and Rühmkorf (n 97) 4.
58. Strauss, 'Unfree Again' (n 93) 191.
59. Anderson, 'Precarious Work' (n 75) 69.
60. Davies (n 6) 97.
61. Carens (n 15) 438.
62. Fudge, 'Illegal Working' (n 60) 583.
63. Strauss, 'Challenging Hegemonic Deregulation?' (n 1) 9. See also Gramsci (1974).
64. Strauss, 'Challenging Hegemonic Deregulation?' (n 1) 4.
65. Attas (n 7) 78.
66. Geddes and Scott (n 88) 28.
67. Rogaly (n 53) 498.
68. Marx (n 103) 492.
69. Strauss, 'Unfree Again' (n 93) 193.
70. Freedland, 'The Contract of Employment' (n 2) 37.
71. Rogaly (n 53) 705.
72. Strauss, 'Challenging Hegemonic Deregulation?' (n 1) 2.
73. Strauss, 'Challenging Hegemonic Deregulation?' (n 1) 2.

Bibliograph

Primary Sources

UK Statutes

Coroners and Justice Act 2009.

Enterprise and Regulatory Reform Act 2013.

Gangmasters Licensing Act 2004.

Human Rights Act 1998.

Immigration Act 2014.

Immigration Act 2016.

Modern Slavery Act 2015.

EU Legislation

European Convention on Human Rights.

UK Cases

Galdikas *v.* Houghton [2016] EWHC 1376 (QB).

Henderson *v.* Dorset Healthcare [2018] EWCA Civ 1841.

Holman *v.* Johnson (1775) 1 Cowp 341.

Hounga *v.* Allen [2014] UKSC 47.

Patel *v.* Mirza [2016] UKSC 42.

R *v.* Secretary of State for the Home Department ex parte Simms [1999] UKHL 33.

Tinsley *v.* Milligan [1993] UKHL 3.

EU Cases

Chowdury and Others *v.* Greece App no 21884/15 (ECHR, 30 March 2017).

CN v. UK App no 4239/08 (ECHR, 13 November 2012).

CN and V v. France App no 67724/09 (ECHR, 11 October 2012).

Rantsev v. Cyprus and Russia App no 25965/04 (ECHR, 7 January 2010)

Siliadin v. France App no 73316/01 (ECHR, 26 July 2005).

Van der Mussele *v.* Belgium (1984) 6 EHRR 163.

Van Droogenbroeck v. Belgium (Commission's Report, 9 July 1980).

Secondary Sources

Anderson, B. (2010). Migration, immigration controls and the fashioning of precarious workers. *Work Employment and Society, 24*.

Anderson, B. (2015). Precarious work, immigration and governance. In C.-U. Schierup et al. (Eds), *Migration, precarity, and global governance: Challenges and opportunities for labour*. Oxford: OUP.

Attas, D. (2000). The case of guest workers: Exploitation, citizenship and economic rights.*Research Publica, 6*, 73–78.

Brass, T. (2004). 'Medieval working practices?' British agriculture and the return of the Gangmaster. *The Journal of Peasant Studies, 31*.

Carens J. (2008). Live-in domestics, seasonal workers, and others hard to locate on the map of democracy. *The Journal of Political Philosophy, 16*.

Bogg, A. (2018). Irregular migrants and fundamental social rights: The case of back-pay under the English Law on illegality. In B. Ryan (Ed.), *Migrant labour and the reshaping of employment law*. Hart (forthcoming).

Bogg, A., & Green, S. (2015). Rights are not just for the virtuous: What Hounga means for the illegality defence in the discrimination torts. *Industrial Law Journal, 44*.

Davies, A. (2014). Migrant workers in agriculture: A legal perspective. In M. Freedland & C. Costello (Eds.), *Migrants at work*. Oxford: OUP.

Doob, C. (2003). *Social inequality and social stratification in US society*. London: Pearson Education.

Favell, A. (2008). The new face of East–West migration in Europe.*Journal of Ethnic and Migration Studies, 34*.

Freedland, M. (2016). The contract of employment and the paradoxes of precarity. *Oxford Legal Studies Research Paper, 37*.

Fudge, J. (2018a). Modern slavery, unfree labour and the labour market: The social dynamics of legal. *Social & Legal Studies, 27*.

Fudge, J. (2018b). Illegal working, migrants and labour exploitation in the UK. *Oxford Journal of Legal Studies, 38*, 557–574.

Geddes, A., & Scott S. (2010). UK food business' reliance on low-wage migrant labour: A case of choice or constraint?In M. Ruhs & B. Anderson (Eds), *Who needs migrant workers: Labour shortages, immigration and public policy*. Oxford: OUP.

Gramsci, A. (1974). *Selections from the prison notebooks* (Q. Hoare & G. Smith, Trans). London: Lawrence and Wishart.

LeBaron, G., & Rühmkorf, A. (2017). The domestic politics of corporate accountability legislation: Struggles over the 2015 UK Modern Slavery Act. *Socio-Economic Review, 12*. Retrieved from https://academic.oup.com/ser/advance-article/doi/10.1093/ser/mwx047/4683730. Accessed on February 5, 2019.

Mantouvalou, V. (2015). "Am i free now?": Overseas domestic workers in slavery. Retrieved from http://discovery.ucl.ac.uk/1468883/3/Mantouvalou_RevisedJLSsubmission%20%28CLAWS00374%27s%20conflicted%20copy%202015-05-06%29.pdf. Accessed on February 5, 2019.

Mantouvalou, V. (2018). The UK Modern Slavery Act 2015 three years on. *Modern Law Review, 81*.

Martin-Ortega, O. (2017). Human rights risks in global supply chains: Applying the UK Modern Slavery Act to the public sector. *Global Policy, 8*.

Marx, K. (1990). *Capital: A critique of political economy* (Vol.1). London: Penguin Classics.

Paz-Fuchs, A. (2016). Badges of modern slavery. *The Modern Law Review, 79.*

Rogaly, B. (2008). Intensification of workplace regimes in British horticulture: The role of migrant workers. *Population Space Place, 14.*

Sassen, S. (1988). *The mobility of labour and capital.* Cambridge, MA: CUP.

Strauss, K. (2009). *Challenging hegemonic deregulation? The UK Gangmaster Licensing Authority as a model for the regulation of casual work.* University of Oxford Working Papers in Employment, Work and Finance. Retrieved from http://citeseerx.ist.psu.edu/viewdoc/download?doi=10.1.1.539.7248&rep=rep1&type=pdf. Accessed on March 4, 2019.

Strauss, K. (2013). Unfree again: Social reproduction, flexible labour markets and the resurgence of Gang Labour in the UK.*Antipode, 45.*

Surak, K. (2013). Guestworkers: A taxonomy. *New Left Review, 84.*

Van Ostaijen, M., Reeger, U., & Zelano, K. (2017). The commodification of mobile workers in Europe – A comparative perspective on capital and labour in Austria, the Netherlands and Sweden.*Comparative Migration Studies, 5.*

Government Publications

Agricultural Workers Rights. Retrieved from https://www.gov.uk/agricultural-workers-rights. Accessed on March 3, 2019.

Gangmaster and Labour Abuse Authority.What we do. Retrieved from http://www.gla.gov.uk/who-we-are/what-we-do/. Accessed on January 2, 2019.

Gangmasters Licensing Authority and Others. (2014, April 9). Tougher enforcement action and stronger penalties for unscrupulous employers. Retrieved from https://www.gov.uk/government/news/tougher-enforcement-action-and-stronger-penalties-for-unscrupulous-employers. Accessed on March 4, 2019.

The Home Office and the Department for Food and Rural Affairs.New Pilot Scheme to bring 2,500 seasonal workers to UK farms. Retrieved from https://www.gov.uk/government/news/new-pilot-scheme-to-bring-2500-seasonal-workers-to-uk-farms. Accessed on March 3, 2019.

The Home Office, Bradley, K., & May, T. (2015, March 26). Historic law to end modern slavery passed. Retrieved from https://www.gov.uk/government/news/historic-law-to-end-modern-slavery-passed. Accessed on March 5, 2019.

HC Deb 1 December 2015, vol 603, cols 175–181.

Hyland, K. (2018, May 4). Letter of Resignation. Retrieved from https://assets.publishing.service.gov.uk/government/uploads/system/uploads/attachment_data/file/708125/20180504_IASC.PDF. Accessed on February 3, 2019.

May, T. (2016, July 31). Defeating modern slavery. Retrieved from https://www.gov.uk/government/news/historic-law-to-end-modern-slavery-passed. Accessed on February 5, 2019.

Modern Slavery (Transparency in Supply Chains) Bill [HL] (2016–17) 105.

Secretary of State for the Home Department, The UK's Future Skills-Based Immigration System (White Paper, Cm 9722, 2018). Retrieved from https://assets.publishing.service.gov.uk/government/uploads/system/uploads/attachment_data/file/766465/The-UKs-future-skills-based-immigration-system-print-ready.pdf. Accessed on March 1, 2019.

Work and Pensions Committee.*Victims of Modern Slavery* (HC 2016-2017, 803-XII).

Reports

Bance, A., & Poinasamy, K. (2009). *Turning the tide: How to best protect workers employed by Gangmasters, five years after Morecambe Bay*. Oxfam Briefing Paper 11. Retrieved from https://oxfamilibrary.openrepository.com/bitstream/handle/10546/114054/bp-turning-tide-morecombe-bay-290709-en.pdf?sequence=1. Accessed on February 2, 2019.

Business and Human Rights Resource Centre. (2017). FTSE 100 at the Starting Line: An analysis of company statements under the UK Modern Slavery Act (p. 2). Retrieved from https://business-humanrights.org/sites/default/files/documents/FTSE%20100%20Modern%20 Slavery%20Act.pdf. Accessed on March 14, 2019.

Chammartin, G., & Taran, P. (2003). *Getting at the roots: Stopping exploitation of migrant workers by organised crime* (p. 2). International Labour Organisation. Retrieved from https://www.ilo.org/wcmsp5/groups/public/--ed_protect/--protrav/--migrant/documents/publication/wcms_232364.pdf. Accessed on March 5, 2019.

International Labour Conference. (2004). Towards a fair deal for migrant workers in the global economy (p. 10). Retrieved from https://www.ilo.org/public/english/standards/relm/ilc/ilc92/pdf/rep-vi.pdf. Accessed on March 17, 2019.

International Labour Office. (2006). International labour migration and development: The ILO perspective (p. 5). Retrieved from https://www.unhcr.org/450665ac2.pdf. Accessed on February 3, 2019.

Phillips, A., & Trautrims, A. (2018). *Agriculture and Modern Slavery Act Reporting: Poor performance despite high risks*. (E. Kenway, ed.). Retrieved from https://www.antislaverycommissioner.co.uk/media/1220/modern-slavery-act-and-agriculture-poor-performance-briefing.pdf. Accessed on March 1, 2019.

The hostile environment for immigrants: How Theresa May has created an underclass in the UK. (2018). *Global Justice Now*. Retrieved from https://www.globaljustice.org.uk/sites/default/files/files/resources/hostile_environment_briefing_feb_2018.pdf. Accessed on January 21, 2019.

Websites and Blogs

Byrne, H. (2018). Modern Slavery and the hostile environment. *Joint Public Issues*, August 3. Retrieved from http://www.jointpublicissues.org.uk/modern-slavery-and-the-hostile-environment/. Accessed on February 14, 2019.

Burland, P. (2017). Smoke but no fire: How not to read UK Government Trafficking Statistics. *Open Democracy*, April 28. Retrieved from https://www.opendemocracy.net/beyondslavery/patrick-burland/smoke-but-no-fire-how-not-to-read-uk-government-trafficking-statistics. Accessed on March 4, 2019.

Ishibashi, L. (2019). Time for a firewall: Ensuring safe reporting for victims of exploitation. *Labour Exploitation*, February 19. Retrieved from https://www.labourexploitation.org/news/time-firewall-ensuring-safe-reporting-victims-exploitation?fbclid=IwAR098jP1aRn38nVkqp777IIgip2TXL1o0bAkZbt7OOuuPS_HdbDjYKVbxG4. Accessed on February 2, 2019.

Kenway, E. (2018). FLEX on Brexit: Government must protect migrant farm workers from exploitation. *Labour Exploitation*, November 15. Retrieved from https://labourexploitation.org/news/flex-brexit-government-must-protect-migrant-farm-workers-exploitation. Accessed on February 3, 2019.

Newspaper Articles

Robinson, C. (2015). The UK's New Immigration Bill creates perfect conditions for slavery to thrive. *The Guardian*, August 28. Retrieved from https://www.theguardian.com/global-development/2015/aug/28/slavery-uk-immigration-act-2014-hostile-environment-undocumented-migrants-focus-on-labour-exploitation-flex. Accessed on February 8 2019.

Multimedia

Broomfield, N. (2006). Ghosts.

SECTION 2

THE POLITICAL ECONOMY AND COMMODIFICATION OF MIGRATION

CHAPTER 5

TO WHAT EXTENT DID THE PRIVATE HYBRIDITY OF THE EAST INDIA COMPANY RESULT IN LACK OF ACCOUNTABILITY?

Akosua-Rose Oppon

ABSTRACT

The East India Company was a hybrid corporation. This hybridity refers to the merchant-state function of the Company, designed as a joint-stock corporate established to trade and make profit, whilst simultaneously exercising public state governance over India. As the Company strived for profits, this was inherently detrimental to ruling a state of people. Its increasing public role alienated both Indians and the British government as it faced increasing criticism. Eventually British state intervention increased until the Company operated as an agent for British imperialism, and its corporate status continued to decline until the Company was replaced by British rule. Ultimately, the legacy of the East India Company represents the incompatibility of private actors taking on state responsibility.

Keywords: Accountability; East India Company; Imperialism; Colonialism; British; impeachment

1. INTRODUCTION

This chapter identifies the metamorphosis of the East India Company ('the Company') as a private corporation to a hybrid body that simultaneously operated as a state. Firstly, the origins of the Company as a private corporation which

Privatisation of Migration Control: Power without Accountability?
Studies in Law, Politics, and Society, Volume 86B, 77–90

Published under exclusive licence by Emerald Publishing Limited
ISSN: 1059-4337/doi:10.1108/S1059-43372021000086B006

also possessed dormant characteristics of a sovereign are explored. Secondly, the chapter follows the Bengal Revolution and its significance to the rise of the Company to a state power. This led to increased state intervention until the Company operated as an agent of the government. Finally, this chapter explores the strengths and shortcomings of the Impeachment trial of Warren Hastings and the consequent transition to a more moralistic, as opposed to profitable, approach in colonial rule.

2. ORIGINS

The initial and prevailing discourse from imperial scholars determines the Company was not an intentional precursor to empire, rather they were merchants that stumbled into ruling. Muir (1923) sums it up as 'Never was Empire less the result of design than the British Empire of India' (p. 2). But more contemporary academia has challenged this narrative, adopting the view that from its inception the foundations of empire would be established through the Company (Stern, 2008, pp. 253–255). Thus, state powers existed from inception, but were merely asserted later (Dirks, 2006, p. 171).

2.1. Monopoly

The establishment of the 1600 Charter was the first concerted effort to capitalise on the Indies. European trade in this region was already firmly established, evidenced by the subsequent exclusion of the Company from Indonesia's trade after the clash with the Deutsch at Amboina (Robins, 2007, pp. 31–46).

The Charter gave the Company exclusive trading rights which represented a partial public interest in foreign trade (Robins, 2012, p. 30). The Charter was subject to renewal after 15 years, and its impermanence recognised that the Company had to consistently prove its profitability for renewal (Robins, 2012).

Given the risks associated with a new emerging market, a monopoly granted by the Charter to the Company was relatively uncontroversial because this mitigated a lot of the risks and allowed the Company to control who could profit in the trade. Smith, a critic of the Company's monopoly, did not dispute the necessity of a charter because it granted monopoly to tradesmen who were exploring a new uncertain trade (Seth, 2012, pp. 221–224). However, he believed the potential monopoly would prevent adequate accountability (Dirks, 2006, pp. 136–138). It appears that monopoly represented despotism by reserving profits to the few.

If the Company had trade exclusivity, profit could be kept high for shareholders (Dirks, 2006, p. 140). As the government alone, a separate entity, had power to renew the Charter, this should have proven effective to hold the Company accountable (Seth, 2012, pp. 221–224). Instead the Company was able to manipulate the government to secure their rights (Seth, 2012, pp. 221–224). For example, when the Charter was not renewed in 1653, Cromwell was forced to submit to the Company's demands when the Company threatened to go into liquidation (Robins, 2012, p. 48). Also, during the political upheaval of the Glorious Revolution, it emerged that the Company was bribing government officials to support renewal of the Charter (Dirks, 2006, p. 141). Furthermore, after a period of intense politicking between the Crown and Parliament concerning the monopolies, a new Company was formed which also had rights to trading in the Indies (Bohun, 1993, p. 63). However, through various means a joint venture was championed by the Company to bring both companies into a single dominant entity and retain monopolisation (Dirks, 2006, p. 141).

2.2. Quasi-governmental Powers

The Charter established privileges typically exclusive to government, such as the right to exercise law and order and mint its own coins (Seth, 2012, pp. 221—-223). These privileges were distinguishable from those possessed by their European competitors in trade with the East. Whilst other nations had a state-led or public–private model, Britain created the Company under the illusion of a private model but with an implicit public agenda (Robins, 2012, p. 23). The public element derived from the intention that its riches would benefit the Commonwealth. These seeds for sovereign power were planted in the Charters and came to be relied on to make laws, declare war and sentence offenders by the Company (Stern, 2008, pp. 253–263).

The grounds for these powers were enflamed with anti-Islamic rhetoric, which provided justification for the Company to transcend the boundaries of legal powers normally afforded to corporations (Stern, 2008, pp. 253–262), and strive for absolute sovereign power divorced from the state (Stern, 2008, pp. 253–263). The Company used its quasi-governmental powers to increase its sovereignty in order to pursue profit-making aims, such as power to wage war and exercise justice in Indian settlements (Robins, 2012, p. 32). For example, military powers were key to the Company's successes against the Portuguese (Dirks, 2006, pp. 140–141).

Whilst these sovereign powers were issued to ensure the Company's success, the Company capitalised on these powers to self-constitute governmental authority. The Company went so far as to use its law-making powers to assert legitimacy over the Crown, the source of the its powers. The Company even believed its law to be superior over British law in its Indian settlements (Stern, 2011, p. 173). It was implicitly held and actioned on that 'English laws reach no further than England' ... and the Charter gave 'absolute' judgment for governance (Stern, 2011).

Similarly, the government granted the ability of the East India Company to conduct diplomacy. The treaties granted by Indo-Persian rulers were highly sought after. Although there was a misunderstanding on their application, they essentially supplemented the Charter rights and even grew to become sources of power in the own right (Stern, 2008, pp. 253–264).

While the Charters emboldened the Company to take rights in India, simultaneously the Company utilised Mughal grants against the government to undermine their authority (Stern, 2008, p. 267).When the British government went to secure Surat under a 'new' Company, the Company defiantly refused to concede to the British government on the authority of Mogul treaties (Stern, 2008). Despite the rising dominance of the Company, the intricate web of diplomacy led to a wide degree of deference from the government to the Company (Stern, 2008, p. 270).

Fundamentally, from its inception the Company was granted wide sovereign powers that initially derived from the British government but came to have a life of their own. These powers were afforded to make the Company more efficient and mitigate the risks from an uncertain market. Although the Charter was intended to bring the Company under control, its state powers alienated the British government and asserted the Company itself as a governing body abroad. Initially there was deference to the Company because of their established diplomatic network, but Britain would later become more interventionist as the Company became more politically sovereign.

2.3. Significance of the Joint-stock Company

The Company was unique and innovative in its organisational form from other European companies; it was implemented as a Joint-stock Company. Trade to the Indies were conducted initially through separate joint-stocks for each journey, but eventually realised in permanency as a corporation in 1657 (Robins, 2012, p. 24).

The joint-stock mechanism provided a platform for risky commercial dealings because the profit derived from management instead of trade (Robins, 2012, p. 26). This benefitted the government in a commercial context, but once the Company had grown in sovereignty whilst chained to the 'the mercies of these Joint-Stock rulers' (Robins, 2012, p. 185), state intervention became more necessary to avoid public moral outrage for the oppression of Indian subjects. Eventually the necessity for accountability became indisputable after the impeachment trial of Warren Hastings (Robins, 2012, p. 186).

Incorporation of a Joint-stock Company entailed a number privileges and duties. Expeditions to the Indian continent were expensive and therefore incorporating the ventures as joint-stock companies was an efficient structure to garner a huge amount of funding through the investment of a mass of shareholders. A joint-stock vehicle mitigated risks because capital could be pooled from passive investors (Shareholders) and potential losses were limited to the scope each had invested in the Company because of limited liability (Robins, 2012, p. 24).

The governance of the Company was separated from the members who possessed a financial stake. Shareholders contributed capital in return for a proprietary interest in the form of shares which determined the proportion of dividends received. Because those with shares were not responsible for management, strategic business decisions were limited to elected officials instead of thousands of shareholders (Robins, 2012, p. 24). This was distinguishable from conventional partnerships of merchants because the management was separated from ownership and delegated to a 'court' of 24 directors, supporting staff and Governors of presidencies (Seth, 2012, pp. 221–225). Whilst this separation between control, on the part of Directors, and ownership, on the part of the shareholders, was more efficient than the traditional model, this also meant that those in control had the scope for opportunistic strategising (Seth, 2012, p. 221).

Smith (2003) first explored the principal-agent problem of the Joint-stock Company when he wrote that the organisation carried inherent 'negligence [and] profusion' (p. 957). Because the managers did not have ownership in the Company, and accordingly no proprietary interest, they were more inclined to pursue objectives incompatible with its owners because they were not bargaining with their own property (Seth, 2012, pp. 221–226). The principal-agent problem was exasperated between the management in India and London, conceptualised by Seth (2012) as 'information asymmetry' (p. 227). Since the average sailing time was six months to India, Directors were usually six months behind affairs (Marshall, 1968, p. 29). This information asymmetry was key to the Company's increasing public-private hybridity. Unsynchronised Company management contributed to an objective conflict between Governors of the Indian subcontinent and the London-based Board of Directors. The Directors' objectives were to maximise trade, however Company officials had incentives to carry out expansionist wars which granted them access to treasuries to personally accumulate wealth (Seth, 2012, pp. 221–231). Corruption was also unchallenged because shareholders were relatively naive to the functioning of the Company. Their interest was purely financial, and any losses would be limited to their share in the Company (Seth, 2012, p. 226).

Although the Company was private and maximised profits for shareholders, the joint-stock vehicle gave the Company potential mechanisms to develop into a state by establishing a legal personality, a constitution and governance of a board of directors (Kemal, 1957, p. 144). Furthermore, the organisational structure of the Joint-stock Company gave way to opportunism. Company officials were able to further exploit the communication asymmetry with Directors in order to pursue imperial aims disjunct from maximising profits. The joint-stock mechanism further exacerbated the lack of accountability because the management was distinct from those who had ownership rights. Furthermore, although the Company was mainly concerned with trade and maximising profits, Company officials could explore imperial aims with little consequence because they were said to be establishing the foundations for British rule (Seth, 2012, pp. 221–231), while contradictorily alienating the British government from its participating in its affairs. (Stern, 2008, p. 283).

3. MANIFESTATION OF STATE POWERS WITHOUT STATE RESPONSIBILITY

The Company morphed from a commercial private corporation to a sovereign in charge of a nation, finally becoming an agent of British rule in India to secure a profit for shareholders in return for the administration of the territories (Robins, 2007, pp. 63–64). This section explores the factors behind the transformation of the Company to a sovereign, namely the manipulation of the Anglo-French rivalry and the role of Robert Clive in the Bengal Revolution. The latter part identifies the outcome of this transformation and state intervention.

The events of the Bengal Revolution are as followed; after securing Madras, Clive addressed Siraj-ud-Daula's takeover at Calcutta in 1756 (Lawson, 1993, p. 89). It would later be called 'the Black Hole' and evoke moral outrage for Britons (Lawson, 1993, p. 89). The remaining Mughal leader armed with support also failed to challenge the Company (Lawson, 1993, p. 77). Later, the Company won at Buxar in 1764 (Lawson, 1993), and were granted land revenue rights (Lawson, 1993, p. 78).

3.1. Anglo-French Rivalry

Prior to the Bengal Revolution, the French Company was the most significant threat, both economically and militaristically. However, the extent of the threat was exaggerated to grant a wide degree of deference to the Company to deploy military power. By framing the Company's conquests against the nation's rivals, it evaded scrutiny for declaring war. Notwithstanding the rivalry between the nations, the respective companies also competed in India. The Company already established coastal settlements (Marshall, 1968, p. 17), but sought Bengal as it was the richest province (Robins, 2012, p. 64). The French Company posed a serious threat (Robins, 2012, p. 68), as French factories strained the Company's operations (Chaudhury, 2017, p. 199). The French thrived at the expense of the Company (Chaudhury, 2017), evidenced by the French Governor-General boasting, 'I made the English tremble for they saw their commerce dwindling' (Chaudhury, 2017, p. 198).

But commercial interests heightened the rivalry between the nations. British and French conflicts bled into the rivalry in India, especially because the French Company was a public body directly ordered by the French government (Mukherjee, 1955, p.77). By exaggerating the French threat, the Company gained governmental support to embark on expensive battles (Lawson, 1993, p. 91). By 1755 the Company was ahead of the French Company, who was less readily supported on the military front (Mukherjee, 1955, p. 79). Furthermore, when the French and British went to war in 1744 the French Company requested the neutrality of the English Company in India, but this was rejected as the states' conflict was seen as as opportunity to further the Company's own ends (Mukherjee, 1955, p. 69).

Rivalry with France drove the Company's ambitions for political and territorial domination in India, including exploiting domestic conflicts between Indian rulers (Mukherjee, 1955, p. 66). This climate birthed military figures such as Clive (Macaulay, 1848, p. 205).

3.2. Militarism, Political Chicanery and Ambition of Clive

The reputation for tactical fighting elevated Robert Clive's status as a military leader (Robins, 2012, p. 70), and led to his success at Buxar (Robins, 2012, p. 77). His militaristic ambition was heralded (Lawson, 1993, p. 87), as they believed commercial pursuits were obtained 'at the point of the sword' (Mukherjee, 1955, p. 17).

However, his skill at political manipulation proved to be the decisive factor for the victory at Plassey (Mukherjee, 1955, p. 80). His strategic engagement with regional politics was also decisive in territorial gains (MacGregor, 2018, p. 28). As Mughal rule declined, the subcontinent was increasingly divided for the Company to exploit factions (MacGregor, 2018, p. 29). The British believed the Company was dragged into Indian politics, but the Company was an enthusiastic participant when presented with an opportunity to gain wealth.

Although Clive was concerned with the profitability of the Company, his contribution was primarily motivated by self-interest and personal ambition (Lawson, 1993, p. 89). His foray into politics was disastrous (Lawson, 1993), and his lifestyle as a *nabob* had led him into financial debt (Lawson, 1993). His return to India was driven by desire for redemption (Joseph, 2010, p. 4). He was always motivated by personal gain, and there was no grand scheme to building empire (Joseph, 2010, p. 3). But when his selfish ambitions came under scrutiny, this narrative changed and became a 'metaphor for both the trajectory of the imperial state' (Joseph, 2010).

After Clive, India became a moral burden for Britain (Joseph, 2010, p. 5). Hence, his actions were subsumed into a wider narrative of British victory in spite of virulent corruption and greed (Joseph, 2010). Macauley starkly reminds us that 'he considered himself as the general not of the Crown but of the Company' (Macaulay, 1848, p. 175). Yet when he came under trial he reiterated 'I have done services to my country' (Marshall, 1968, p. 171). Any larger narrative to construct him as part of the nation was manipulative.

Clive's legacy is dichotomous. He resurrected Company honour yet became notorious for the pillaging of Indians and suspiciously amassing wealth (Joseph, 2010). He further shows the shortcomings of the hybridity of the Company. Clive's pursuit of profit and power ultimately furthered the downfall of the Company, due to his exploitation of the sovereign diplomatic and military powers. This would ultimately lead the Company to become a state ruler. Furthermore, the Company's criticisms were repeatedly justified under a patriotic narrative.

3.3. Initial Prosperity Post-revolution

Successes of Bengal fuelled the belief that shareholders would face increased dividends from the plunder (Bowen, 2009, p. 57). Consequently, the value of stock tripled in 1766 to over £4 million (Bowen, 2009, p. 58). Excitement was whipped so feverishly, that shareholders met in London to vote the dividend increase for 16 hours (Robins, 2012, p. 79). In the six years following conquest, the wealth drained from Bengal estimated £20 million in revenues for the Company (Robins, 2012).

3.4. Initial Concerns

Clive presented a dilemma for Company officials; there was a reluctance to assume the responsibility of a political sovereign, yet the financial advantages presented lucrative potential (Lawson, 1993, p. 100). Concerns were raised about the involvement of the Crown's army after Plassey, because the British government was apprehensive to be dragged into future wars (Bowen, 2009, p. 72). Thus, risk was mitigated by appointing a Crown Plenipotentiary in 1769 (Bowen, 2009).

Amongst the British elite, there were concerns for the Company's growing powers and a desire for state involvement. Cowper, an influential poet, expressed the sentiment of many when he said '[the Company] has ruled with a rod of iron, to which it is impossible they should have a right … that government therefore is bound to interfere' (Marshall, 1968, pp. 150–151).

Although there was general disapproval of the situation, the government was reluctant to take up the mantle of governance in India. Instead, plans began to relegate the Company to an agent of the state (Marshall, 1968, p. 117).

3.5. The Downfall

Domestically, the textile industry first suffered. Before, weavers were economically stable, but under Company rule they were reduced to working as slaves (Robins, 2012, p. 80). The economic violence reduced many skilled workers to self-mutilation (Robins, 2012, p. 81). Additionally, famines dramatically worsened (Robins, 2012, p. 93). Company servants began to horde grain (Robins, 2012, p. 94), tax revenues continued to be collected and no relief was provided (Robins, 2012, p. 95). Britain believed the Company was responsible for the death of one-third of the population yet modern conservative data suggests 1.2 million (Robins, 2012). This presented the first morally repugnant conflict between the private and public duties of the Company.

Private trade declined and political power increased leading to confusion (Lawson, 1993, p. 103). Military force became a vital part of Company operations and merchants were side-lined (Robins, 2012, p. 97). By 1770, there was a consensus amongst Directors that Bengal was 'a hollow acquisition' with precarious revenues (Robins, 2012, p. 99).

By 1772, the Company had 'a long-overdue repayment of a £300,000 short-term loan from the Bank of England, along with nearly £1,000,000 in unpaid taxes' (Robins, 2012, p. 100). The Company resorted to requesting loans from the government (Robins, 2012), giving the government grounds to intervene. The financial crises of Company rendered them obliged to heed to government scrutinisation (Bowen, 2009, p. 71).

3.6. State Intervention and Legislation

The government was forced to bail out the Company with £1.4 million and introduced legislation to restore the profitability of the Company (Sramek, 2011, p. 26). The 1773 Regulating Act made the Company's territorial acquisition formally owned by the Crown, and introduced a Governor-General to administer the Presidencies (MacGregor, 2018, p. 29). The Governor-General was responsible for disciplining the Company and enforcing orders from Parliament (Marshall, 1968, p. 113). Warren Hastings became the first Governor-General (Marshall, 1968, p. 115), and he was explicitly prohibited from accepting gifts (Marshall, 1968, p. 153 (section xxiii)). The role of Governor-General was a crown appointment (Wilson, 2016, p. 133), and had extensive powers to veto decisions by the Bengal Council (Lawson, 1993, p. 128). This attempt to curb Company power had laid the foundation for later despotism, even though this reform was framed as progressive.

Furthermore, Lord North reformed the electoral system to allow for continuity in the management of the Company. Voting powers decreased so that power was concentrated in the hands of few (Bowen, 2009, pp. 70–71). This aimed to reduce any threats to political stability (Bowen, 2009, p. 71). Pitt's India Act 1784 established a Board of Control which began a gradual progression of state control over the military and revenue affairs in India (Bowen, 2009, p. 73). Furthermore, the Act removed the power of the General Court to overturn the Director's decisions that had been backed by the Board of Control (Bowen, 2009, pp. 75–76). This widened further distinction of ownership and control in the Joint-stock Company, because shareholders had virtually no say in the Company's administration in India (Bowen, 2009, p. 76). Following Pitt's India Act, instead of being accountable to shareholders, the management of the Company was now accountable to the Board of Control for administrative matters and required their approval (Bowen, 2009, p. 77).

Despite initial qualms over state intervention, the legislation benefitted shareholders (Robins, 2012, p. 25). Statutory regulations meant 'institutional metamorphosis' in the Company (Bowen, 2009, p. 83). No longer an independent entity, the Company became an agent of imperial government which served national interests as well as corporate profit concerns (Bowen, 2009).

In conclusion, after Bengal Revolution, the Company became the merchant-state. The public–private hybridity of the Company proved unstable, which required government intervention. However, India remained primarily under the rule of the Company, who harboured separate interests from the government. This dynamic demonstrated a lack of accountability because the Company became too big to fail; its private functions became too complex and vital to the economy for a public overhaul. Instead, increasing intervention made the Company an agent.

4. IMPEACHMENT TRAIL OF WARREN HASTINGS BY EDMUND BURKE 1788–1795

This section explores the trial of Warren Hastings. In his prosecution, Burke referred to the universalism in divine natural law through the reiteration of religion and the supremacy of morality. He supplemented this with hyperbole to evoke British sympathy to recognise the plights of India as an affront to British honour. Additionally, the criticisms and outcome of the trial are analysed. Namely, Burke did not adequately challenge imperialism as an ideology, his legal arguments were inconsistent, and his evocation of sympathy alienated his arguments. Although he did not win the trial, the high-profile nature of the case marked a turning point for the Company's accountability to the state. Following the trial, the Company was subsumed under the nation's imperial ambitions and a commitment to modernising the colonised peoples began under 'imperial self-legitimation' (Kaul, 2009, pp. 120–123).

4.1. Challenging Legality with Natural Law

Burke built his case on natural law which relied on the religious uprightness of British society to hold the Company accountable. This was because the black-letter legal framework was insufficient to address the hybridity of the Company, leaving Burke to resort to a higher form of law.

Natural law went beyond the legal framework which was insufficient to address the incompatibility of a simultaneously sovereign and private corporation

(Maxwell, 2015, p. 46). From its very inception, a 'delegation of the whole power and sovereignty of this kingdom [was] sent into the East' (Marshall & Todd, 1991, p. 283). Burke highlighted the incompatibility of the Company as ruler because as a private trading corporation with a public role, they were governing in the interests of shareholders and not those governed (Marshall, 1968, p. 67). This was demonstrated by imputing a moral obligation derived from natural law (Marshall, 1968, p. 67). Further, he referred to Roman law to demonstrate the incompatibility of public and private functions (Marshall & Todd, 1991, p. 283), which he believed English law insufficiently addressed.

The universalism of natural law countered Hastings' claim to 'geographical morality' (Marshall & Todd, 1991, p. 346); as he was outside English jurisdiction, Hastings claimed he could legitimately use discretion because India was governed arbitrarily. This 'geographical morality' was a scathing criticism against Hastings' claim to be outside the rule of law (Maxwell, 2015, p. 47). Burke claimed natural law was universal and therefore Hastings could not escape it (Maxwell, 2015). Yet legal principles on morality were also insufficient. Although it evoked emotional responses to the morally repugnant behaviour of the Company, ultimately it was insufficient to meet the standards of legal precision required by the House of Lords (Maxwell, 2015, p. 57).

Burke knew that British uprightness was rooted in its fervent claims to Christian faith, compared to the 'prejudices and absurdities' of Asiatic religions (Marshall, 1968, p. 190). Burke looked to the divinity 'which governs all law – the law of our Creator' (Marshall, 1968, p. 177) which entrenched protection under the rule of law indiscriminately (Marshall, 1968). Burke knew that if his legal principles aligned with Christianity, a refutation would reveal the hypocrisy of Company men who also aligned themselves with Christianity. Furthermore, natural law combatted the white supremacy complex that a lower form of justice should be applied to Indians (Robins, 2012, p. 140).

4.2. Moral Urgency and Sympathy

Using sympathy, Burke appealed to the paternalism of Britain to be protective over their Indian subjects. Consequently, Britain was constructed as a saviour to redeem its people from the illegality of Company rule.

Sympathy provided the undercurrent to his natural law argument (Sramek, 2011). Burke pierced his legal arguments with moral urgency and theatrics. In recounting the acts of Rajah Devi Singh, an official appointed by Hastings, he embellished the brutality imposed by the Rajah on the town of Rangpur (Wilson, 2016, p. 150). He aimed to appeal to emotions by emphasising the victimhood of Indians. As this reasoning offered no signficant legal weight, this demonstrates Burke was more concerned with winning public opinion over a successful prosecution. (Maxwell, 2015, p. 53). In the long-term this was strategic because the public had greater influence to pressure their parliamentary representatives to address their foreign policy in India.

Furthermore, Burke evoked sympathy from the public as a tool to garner support for his cause (Maxwell, 2015, p. 61). As Indians were believed to be racially inferior (Sramek, 2011, p. 12), sympathy was an important tool to establish a 'common condition of humanity' (Maxwell, 2015, p. 64). This could bridge the gap between the dispassionate white public and Indians (Maxwell, 2015, p. 62).

The outcome of the trial, although unsuccessful, marked a turning point for British policy in India. The Company gained institutional legitimacy as a conduit for British affairs (Kent, 2014, p. 32), only when framed as a public good as opposed to serving commercial interests. Before, the private corporation claimed independence and fought against state intervention, but the trial was significant in forming the agency relationship that followed. Its hybridity, now institutionally legitimised, was no longer accountable to the state but rather seen as an extension of the state.

4.3. Criticism of the Trial: Attack on Company and Not Conquest

A fundamental flaw was that Burke's condemnation of the Company did not go far enough to condemn imperialism in its entirety (Sramek, 2011, p. 34). By making Hastings the figurehead of all crime in India and leveraging a personal attack, the wider misgivings in India from the Company were normalised and dismissed (Sramek, 2011). The Corporate entity was redeemed whilst the individual negated (Kent, 2014, p. 36). Burke's moral attack provided an impetus for India to morph into a 'patriotic enterprise' that was 'answerable to the nation' as opposed to the once profiteering shareholders (Dirks, 2006, p. 125). This elevation to an honourable pursuit would actually legitimise colonial rule in India; the empire was raised above scandal (Dirks, 2006, p. 125). Burke was very clear that he did not vindicate empire itself (Dirks, 2006, p. 191). He believed Indians should be free from Company rule, but not British rule altogether (Dirks, 2006, p. 287), suggesting he was also complicit in the white supremacy he fought against. He elevated the humanity of Indians by stating 'their morality is equal to ours … more true morality and wisdom' (Marshall & Todd, 1991, p. 361) whilst contradictorily believing that Company trade with the Indics disturbed the natural order of white supremacy; he stated 'it is not the Englishman, but it is the black Banyan that is the Master' (Marshall & Todd, 1991, p. 293).

4.4. Inconsistencies

Although a great orator, his legal arguments were often inconsistent. His arguments interplayed between the universalism of natural law yet also reiterated that 'law of the Nation' and Indian laws and customs were also to be binding (Maxwell, 2015, p. 47). Therefore, his stance as to what extent natural law should circumvent national customs was questionable. He assumed they work together, but in conflict he does not make clear which should reign supreme (Maxwell, 2015, p. 48). Maxwell exposes Burke's fallacy, stating 'Hastings must be judged by natural law because national/local law is insufficient to grasp his crimes' but also he 'must be judged by national/local laws … essential in resisting the rootless … oppressions of the Company' (Maxwell, 2015).

Pitts (2007), defending Burke, claimed that his appeals to universalism were grounded in local culture and practise (p. 99), instead of working against one another. In this way, we see that natural law grounded in national sentiment could lead Britons to see beyond the limited scope of national laws without questioning their integrity. Pitts (2007) further suggests Burke demonstrated the harmony of national and natural law to curb the nationalism of British supremacy over India (p. 97). Although Pitts presents a strong argument, it remains clear that the inconsistency remains; Burke asserted the supremacy of 'universal' law over national law while also seeking accountability under national law.

4.5. Sympathy

Burke appealed to the public sympathy of the charges brought against the Company. But in reality his 'public' were 'propertied, white, male Britons' (Maxwell, 2015, p. 60). Sympathy did not uplift the Indians to the common humanity he suggested, but rather exoticised Indian suffering as an 'abjected other, as the constitutive exclusion that would cohere its own fantasy of identity' (Rai, 2003, p. 42) This 'sentimental rhetoric' was common in other abolitionist politics (Carey, 2005, p. 19). The effect was to see the plights of oppression as beneath the oppressors.

Burke exaggerated to gather public support. Hastings was described as the 'one in whom all the frauds, all the peculations, all the violence, all the tyranny in India are embodied, disciplined and arrayed' (Marshall & Todd, 1991, pp. 275–276). Furthermore, he extensively detailed the torture inflicted on by the Rajah. Yet his rhetoric did more to alienate his case than support it. His exoticism of Indian suffering was an obtuse provocation of emotion over legal reasoning and he was deeply criticised for it (Maxwell, 2015, p. 68).

Furthermore, the boldness in orations was initially widely regarded, but came to take on such a tone of 'moral ferocity', that it would alienate him from potential supporters (Samet, 2001, p. 399). The more he became embroiled in the case, it seemed less for the public good and rather became a personal vengeance (Samet, 2001, p. 401).

4.6. Conclusion

Burke was instrumental in turning India into a colonial project, where empire was no longer intrinsically immoral if divorced from profits. The burden of virtuous ruling would be taken up in self-afflicted obligation by Britain for them to maintain empire (Sramek, 2011, p. 38). The trial represented a 'ritual sanitization' (Kent, 2014, p. 28) because instead of ending Company rule, it was permitted to go on under the guise of patriotic goodwill. The trial also represents a veil to the end of mercantile corruption yet continued as a 'purified formation … Based on virtue, duty and service' (Kent, 2014, p. 58).

5. FINAL THOUGHTS

This chapter has outlined and explored the metamorphosis of the Company and subsequently its accountability to the state. Although the Company was a private organisation, its hybridity arose from its rise to state power in India.

Consequently, its relationship to the British state changed. Initially the Company was sent to the Indies for trade, but its powers exceeded its role as a private company and provided the foundation for economic and political dominance. At the Bengal Revolution, the Company remained private in name but increasing state intervention reduced it to an agent of the state as it continued to operate as a corporation. Finally, the trial represents the Company's shift to a more public role as Burke demonstrated the incompatibility of a private corporation in governance, and colonial rule became driven by imperial paternalism as well as profits.

BIBLIOGRAPHY

Bohun, J. (1993). Protecting Prerogative: William III and the East India Trade Debate 1689–1698. *Past Imperfect*, *2*, 63.

Bowen, H. V. (2009). *The business of empire: The East India Company and Imperial Britain 1756–1833*. Cambridge: Cambridge University Press.

Carey, B. (2005). *British abolitionism and the rhetoric of sensibility: Writing, sentiment, and slavery 1760–1807*. London: Palgrave Macmillan.

Chaudhury, S. (2017). *Trade, politics and society: The Indian Milieu in the Early Modern Era*. London: Routledge.

Dirks, N. (2006). *The scandal of empire*. Cambridge: Harvard University Press.

Griffiths, P. J. (1946). *The British in India*. London: Northumberland Press Limited.

Joseph, N. (2010). Robert Clive and Imperial Modernity. *12.2 CLCWeb: Comparative Literature and Culture*. doi:doi.org/10.7771/1481-4374.1592

Kaul, S. (2009). Company affairs.*Eighteenth-Century Life*, *33*, 120.

Kemal, R. (1957). 'The Evolution of British Sovereignty in India' 6 Indian Year Book of International Affairs 144.

Kent, E. (2014). *Corporate character: Representing Imperial Power in British India 1786–1901*. Toronto: University of Toronto Press.

Lawson, P. (1993). *The East India Company: A history*. London: Longman Publishing.

Macaulay, T. B. (1848). *Critical and historical essays contributed to the Edinburgh review* (5th ed.).London: Longman, Brown, Green, and Longmans.

MacGregor, A. (2018). *Company curiosities*. London: Reaktion Books.

Marshall, P. J. (1968). *Problems of empire*. London: Allen & Unwin.

Marshall, P. J., & Todd, S. (Eds.). (1991). *The Writings and Speeches of Edmund Burke, Vol. 6: India: The Launching of the Hastings Impeachment: 1786–1788*. Oxford: Oxford University Press.

Maxwell, L. (2015). *Public trials: Burke, Zola, Arendt, and the politics of lost causes*. Oxford: Oxford University Press.

Muir, R. (1923 [1915]). *The making of British India 1756–1858*. London: University of Manchester.

Mukherjee, R. (1955). *The rise and fall of the East India Company* (2nd ed.). Germany: Deutscher Verlag der Wissenschaften.

Mulligan, M. (2018) The East India Company: Non-State Actor as Treaty-Maker. In J. Summers & A. Gough (Eds.) *Non-State Actors and International Obligations: Creation, Evolution and Enforcement* (p. 42). Boston: Brill.

Pitts, J. (2005). *A turn to empire: The rise of Imperial Liberalism in Britain and France*. Princeton, NJ: Princeton University Press.

Rai, A. (2003). *The Rule of Sympathy: Sentiment, race, and power 1750–1850*. London: Palgrave Macmillan.

Robins, N. (2007). This Imperious Company. *Journal of Crohn's and Colitis*, *25*, 31.

Robins, N. (2012). *The corporation that changed the world* (2nd ed.). London: Pluto Books.

Samet, E. (2001). A Prosecutor and a Gentleman: Edmund Burke's idiom of impeachment. *ELH*, *68*, 397.

Seth, V. (2012). The East India Company—A case study in Corporate Governance. *Global Business Review*, *13*, 221.

Smith, A. (2003 [1776]). *The wealth of nations*. New York, NY: Bantam Classics.

Sramek, J. (2011). *Gender, morality, and race in Company India 1765–1858*. London: Palgrave Macmillan.

Stern, P. (2008). "A Politie of Civil & Military Power": Political thought and the late seventeenth-century foundations of the East India Company-State. *Journal of British Studies*, *47*, 253.

Stern, P. (2011). *The Company-state: Corporate Sovereignty and the Early Modern Foundations of the British Empire in India*. Oxford: Oxford University Press.

Wilson, J. (2016). *India conquered: Britain's Raj and the Chaos of Empire*. London: Simon & Schuster.

CHAPTER 6

MIGRATION AS A COMMODITY: DO YOU POSSESS THE 'GOLDEN TICKET…?' AN ASSESSMENT OF THE TIER 1 (INVESTOR) VISA'S SOCIAL AND ECONOMIC EFFECT ON THE UK'S MIGRATION SYSTEM

Isobel Kamber

ABSTRACT

This chapter aims to critically access the Tier 1 (Investor) visa's effect on the conceptualisation of the British Migration system. The scheme offers an exclusive route to temporary residency in the UK in return for a £2 million investment in Britain. It is contended that the government have consistently underestimated the continual detrimental effects of offering such a scheme due to their overarching pursuit for economic gain. As such, the scheme has imparted social disadvantage, highlighting the prevalence of inequality and the existence of a hierarchy of desired migrants. Furthermore, it is asserted that the investor scheme is facilitating threats to the public's safety, exemplified in the recent Salisbury Novichok attacks. However fundamentally, this chapter will seek to illustrate that the Tier 1 (Investor) visa has commodified the UK's migration system, bestowing investors with a 'golden ticket' and in turn disregarding the needs of the UK's citizens.

Keywords: Investor visa; Tier 1; golden ticket; immigration; commodification; investors

Privatisation of Migration Control: Power without Accountability?
Studies in Law, Politics, and Society, Volume 86B, 91–105

ISSN: 1059-4337/doi:10.1108/S1059-43372021000086B007

1. INTRODUCTION

Introduced in 2008, the UK Tier 1 (Investor) Visa, often referred to as the 'golden visa programme' (Tryfonidou, 2017), offers residency in the UK in return for a £2 million investment.[1] This programme has been widely criticised for its 'lack of transparency'; 'inability to return any benefit to UK residents', and for 'transforming the UK into a safe haven for money launderers'. However, the overarching effect of offering such a programme is that the UK's migration system can now be conceptualised as a market, placing the commodity of residency up for sale. In turn, the government has created a metaphorical barrier – able to be lifted with little restraint by any non-European Economic Area (EEA) high-net-worth individual and left closed for the majority: separating the rich from the poor and affirming the existence of a hierarchy of desired migrants (Anderson, 1990) within the UK's nexus of societal values.

This chapter will argue that the existence of the Tier 1 (Investor) Visa is detrimental to the conceptualisation of the migration system and should either be revoked from operation or in the alternative nullified.

In the first part, an outline of the visa requirements will be set out, reviewing both the generalities and irregularities of the visa. These abnormalities – only capable of being conceptualised as problematic – will be discussed with note to Tanasoca's comparison of the programme to the anachronistic buying and selling of honours in Early Stuart England (Tanasoca, 2016, pp. 169–195). In the second part, the government's economic justifications and incentives for promoting such a programme will be discussed, each then being refuted through an illustration of the benefits for the investors themselves. As will be embellished, it is this chapter's contention that the sole substantive benefit is unbalanced, lying not with the UK and instead lying exclusively with investors. The third part will evaluate the lack of transparency that inundates the visa, as is exemplified by the recent *Salisbury Novichok Attacks* and the *Abylazov Fraud*. Here, the neglect of due diligence in the distribution of the visa is argued emblematic of its consistent criticism. The final part submits that the visa is leading to inequality and the affirmation of the hierarchy. As Sandal (2012) so shrewdly notes, 'laws do not only guide action. Markets do not only allocate goods. They all express and promote certain attitudes toward the goods being exchanged'. Hence, it will be argued that, in placing a visa on the market the government promotes the attitude that social and political equality within society is of little to no value. It seems for the government economic gain is their primary, if not, only, pursuit.

2. PART I: WELCOME TO THE UK: MONEY REALLY CAN BUY YOU ANYTHING…

2.1. The (Un)stable Foundations

'In 2008, the UK introduced its (current) golden visa programme, officially known as the Tier 1 (Investor) visa, replacing the previous "Investor Immigrant" category, which was introduced in 1994'.[2] It is true that 1994, was the UK's initial official affirmation that the government felt it was appropriate to place the migration system on the market, yet such principal far exceeds 1994. In fact, many academics have likened the visa to that of the selling of peerages and honours in Early Stuart England, with Tanasoca rebutting the legitimacy of both markets, stating 'money did not make one worthy of noble status. Does money make one worthy of citizenship?'. It is conceded, the UK have not, as of yet, gone so far as to place citizenship on the market. However, to answer whether money makes one worthy of residency, comparisons should be drawn with the result of selling honours. 'Philip Stanhope, convicted for sodomy and pardoned for murder'; 'Robert Lord Rich, a famous pirate'; and even 'Sir William Grey, involved in a customs-evasion scandal' (Mayes, 1957) were all able to purchase honours. Hence, just as 'wealth did not make one a true *gentilhomme*' (Sandal, 2012), wealth conversely does not make one worthy of residency. Not neglecting the fact that the legitimacy of such an assertion is contingent on the limits and restraints of the programme. However, it is such that the lack of limits, restraints and requirements of the visa, epitomise the reality that the visa is solely concerned with the financials of its potential applicants, otherwise referred to as 'prized assets' (Shachar & Hirschl, 2014, pp. 231–257).

As a visa 'designed to encourage high net worth individuals' from non-EEA nations 'to make a substantial financial investment in the UK' (Perrott & Yu, 2018), there is a minimum investment stipulation of £2 million.[3] This should either be invested in 'UK government bonds, share capital or loan capital in active and trading UK registered companies'.[4] Resultantly, the investor makes a purchase 'of 75 points', as is required to gain residency per Appendix A[5] of the Immigration Rules. Yet, despite the uniformity of this visa being distributed under the *Points Based System* alike to all other visas; and the applicant being allegedly subject to all the normal refusal grounds (as is rebutted in Part III of this chapter),[6] it should not be overlooked that the visa provides a fundamental exception to the English Language requirement that all alternative visa's require.[7] What is more, 'the UK rewards those who invest over £5 million or £10 million with an accelerated route to settlement (three and two years, respectively, rather than five)'.[8] This is crucial in exemplifying how the Tier 1 (Investor) visa is manifested purely on the financial ability of potential applicants with disregard for social integration. This stems from the government awarding indefinite leave to remain (ILR) – 'a settled status from which one can proceed to citizenship' (Prahbhat, 2018, p. 38) argued to be a reinforcement of 'a sense of security'; and 'consolidation of legal rights' (Prahbhat, 2018, p. 52) – in exchange for money. Conversely for migrants who do not possess excessive wealth, the process of gaining ILR status is 'difficult' and 'mentally exhausting' (Prahbhat, 2018, p. 120) – a distinct paradox when compared to the simple corporate transaction required of investors under the Tier 1 (Investor) programme.

In sum, for a high-net-worth individual, an application of residency poses the simple question of where to invest. Yet, for the majority of individuals the application for a visa poses a multitude of personal questions and requirements, far beyond the mere materialistic requirement of investment. For example, a Tier 2 (General Worker) visa, requires: 'valid certificate of job sponsorship'[9]; 'proof of an appropriate salary'[10]; 'proof of knowledge of English Language'[11]; 'proof of personal savings'[12]; 'tuberculosis test results'[13] (if you are from a listed country); and finally a 'criminal record certificate for any country you've lived in for 12 months or more'.[14] In comparison to that of the Tier 1 (Investor) visa it is evident the Tier 2 visa requires a multitude of additional requirements. This typifies the investor visa's evident exceptions to normal migratory requirements, substituting any normality for the attribute of wealth in potential applicants.

2.2. Principal or Prominence?

Despite the visa's commodity status, readers of this chapter might question the impact of the visa considering its target market is singularly non-EEA high-net-worth individuals, in other words a minority. The visas acquisition prominence is far below that of alternative visas. As can be illustrated by the 2017 Immigration Statistic Document released by the government, between 2008 and 2016, 3,352 Tier 1 (Investor) Visas had been granted[15] whereas, in the same period, 98,397 Tier 2 (General) visas had been granted.[16] Whilst this is key in illustrating that the visa is not as popular as other visas; a more cogent question is how many of these investors went onto naturalise? This would answer whether an investor regards Britain as a mere commodity (to be purchased and sold) or as a community with the potential to integrate into. However, despite the intrigue, a Freedom of Information request was denied under Section 12 of the Freedom of Information Act 2000, ironically on the ground it exceeded the cost limit per request.[17] Yet, it is these papers contention that the prominence of the visa can be noted irrelevant in the conceptualisation of the migration system itself. Due to it not being the prominence of the visa stamping migration as that of a commodity; but instead its mere existence. It is the mere principal that those falling within namely, the 'one percent' (Keister, 2014, pp. 347–367) possess the ability to purchase residency, which has in turn commodified migration.

3. PART II: INCENTIVES (OR LACK, THEREOF)?

It is a pragmatic assumption that investors can benefit from purchasing the visa, because otherwise there is little doubt purchase would be obsolete. However, the government's justifications for the scheme are fundamentally grounded upon the visa's benefit to the UK economy. Whilst such an argument is easy to adduce (Sandal, 2012), its validity is nonetheless easy to refute – and it seems the real benefit is unmistakeably gained solely by the investor. Meanwhile, the UK suffers social detriment outweighing any trivial economic justification in offering such a programme.

3.1. The United Kingdom's Fictitious Impetus

The government relies on the justification that 'a considerable amount of external funds are brought into the country with a benefit to the banking sector', 'consequently flowing into the economy of the country' as a result of the Tier 1 (Investor) visa. The government goes even further to suggest the 'direct investment into share capital or loan capital in active and trading UK registered companies' (Migration Advisory Committee (MAC), 2018) are of further benefit and thus a justification for the visa.

It is undeniable that this is partially true, however the minimal, even trivial, benefit of these investments does not outweigh the detriment that stems from the visa. Arguments made by Tryfonidou, and MAC reports contend a two-limb argument to this assertion.

Firstly, 'investors predominantly invest in government bonds, which are simply a loan to the UK government'[18] otherwise referred to as 'gilts'. As a 'low risk, safe investment', (MAC) (2018) labelled by Aston (2011) as the 'crème de la crème of low risk investments', the existence of 'gilts' push investors away from 'higher risk but more exciting' and profitable investments, such as private trading companies specialising in 'tech or bio science'. (MAC) (2018) Were investors to more regularly invest into such spheres it would stimulate the UK economy much more directly. However, 'because most regulated financial institutions struggle to value private companies, let alone confirm the market value in writing' (MAC) (2018) this pushes investors away from investing in these more favourable sectors. Put simply, the prevalence of investment in gilts to satisfy the requirements of the visa work by effectively loaning the government money, rather than investing in the UK which is exemplary of the lack of any genuine and substantial benefit the Tier 1 (Investor) visa has on the UK economy.

In relation to the second limb of the argument, the gilts are either sold by the Debt Management Office via 'outright gilt auctions' (United Kingdom Debt Management Office) or through a secondary provider being a stockbroker or even the Bank of England's brokerage service (Rodgers, 1997, pp, 241–247). The MAC note that since

> the government is already able to access the finance it requires from capital markets, particularly at a time when UK gilt auctions are typically oversubscribed, it does not need the additional funding provided by the Tier 1 (Investor) route. (MAC, 2014)

This can only be appraised as an evident reiteration of the 'little benefit' (BBC News, 2018), the visa bears to the UK and its 'citizens' (BBC News, 2018). With rationalisation consistently grounded upon its 'supposed' considerable benefit to the UK economy, it seems the government were, and continue to be, ignorant with regard to how substantial the benefit actual is. Therefore, the impetus for providing such a programme is seemingly fictitious for the UK and its citizens.

3.2. The Dream Investment…

It is conceded investor migrants 'indirect investments' do bring some very minimal benefit to the UK but these are primarily in relation to trivial matters, such as 'household expense' and 'children's education' (MAC, 2018, p. 2) as distinguished by the MAC. Whilst these are all valid forms of trivial investment, the MAC also controversially include 'property acquisition' (MAC, 2018, p. 2) in their list of indirect beneficial investment. It is true that 'housing in particular is a great source of tax revenue for the UK' (MAC, 2018, p. 14) due to the 'substantial charges to Stamp Duty Land Tax'. (MAC, 2018, p. 35) However, it should not be overlooked such a suggestion fails to detect the concealed detriment that investor property acquisition is having on the UK – serving 'to price out local residents from the expensive areas' of Britain via gentrification. (MAC (2018), p. 27) The MAC claim that investor visa migrants 'typically purchase multi-million pound properties to reside in' and as such the committee assert they 'are not pricing ordinary residents out of the market but rather they stimulate the high end property market'. (MAC, 2018, p. 38) However, the MAC seem to have missed the fundamental point that a stimulation of the high end property market, has the 'domino' effect of pushing the whole property market value up due to the economics of supply and demand. Put simply by Stein (1995), housing prices 'correlate with the volume of housing transactions' (pp. 379–406). Hence it should be of concern that 'overseas investors snapped up more than half of all properties for sale in London's most exclusive postcodes in the last half of 2017' hitting its 'highest level in five years' (William, 2018). Whilst, it is true that some of these investors will not possess a Tier 1 (Investor) visa. Nonetheless, one should not ignore that the very existence of the visa, facilitates property acquisition by many non-EEA nationals, (MAC, 2018, p. 14) accordingly adding to the detrimental effect of 'driving up prices and locking millions of UK citizens out of the housing market' (Helm, 2014) much to the MAC's ignorance.

3.3. The European Union and the 'Bootstrapping of the Right to Residence' (Joppke., 2010, p.15)

One should note, the UK is not alone in offering such a programme. Other member states of the European Union (EU) offer programmes comparable to that of the UK. Austria, for example, offers citizenship for 'an investment estimated to exceed €2.5 million' (Joppke) (2010) p. 15 bypassing the requirements of 'prior residence, language or even an interview'. (Joppke) (2010) p. 15 As aforementioned, the UK have not, as of yet, gone so far as to place citizenship on the market. It was noted by Prahbhat that for the UK, citizenship is 'exclusively for those with close links to the UK' (Prahbhat) (2018) operating 'through a mix of territoriality and parentage' (Prahbhat) (2018) as was secured by the 1981 British Nationality Act.

However, the alternative citizenship purchase programmes in fellow EU member states do not operate in a vacuum, and indirect adversity upon the UK is inevitable. This is because per the Treaty on the Functioning of the European Union (TFEU), 'union citizenship' is 'a fundamental status of nationals of EU member states'.[19,20] Ancillary to this, Article 20(2)(a) TFEU instilled 'the right to move and reside freely within the territory of the Member States'.[21]

The existence of such comparable programmes within alternative member states means investors who have purchased citizenship with little constraint, are able to freely enter Britain by virtue of the UK's current membership to the EU. At present, and until the outcome of the UK's imminent exit from the EU through the Brexit process is finalised, the exploitation of EU free movement by high-net-worth individuals who inevitably lack credibility is effortless. As such many European governments have been 'accused of opening the door to criminals through lax sales of passports and visas to the super-rich' (Rankin, 2018) due to a lack of due diligence surrounding the distribution of such investor visas and or citizenship. It seems by virtue of the UK's membership to the EU and consequential acceptance of free movement, the repercussions of the commodification of numerous migration systems, beyond just that of our own, currently stretch far beyond the remit of even the UK's control. However, this is not to say the UK's transparency and due diligence efforts are without critique. In fact, the UK has been heavily criticised for a complete lack of due diligence in their assessment of applications for the Tier 1 (Investor) visa. Hence whilst investor residency might be a 'reliable marker of wealth' (Sandal, 2012), 'we can doubt it is also a reliable marker of good character or civic competence' (Sandal, 2012).

4. PART III: AN OPAQUE TRANSPARENCY

The need for 'higher standards of due diligence' (Sandal, 2012) within the assessment of awarding the visa, has formed a large part of the critique of the programme since its entrance onto the market in 2008. Whilst efforts have been taken to minimise the detrimental effects of the visa, namely, the maximisation of the investment requirement from £1 million to £2 million,[22] these efforts have not been successful enough. And with the overarching prevail of a lack of transparency, the visa continues to pose not just economic concern for UK citizens but also social concern in the form of a threat to public safety.

4.1. The Facilitation of Kremlin Intelligence in Salisbury

The popularity of the visa with Russian investors (Dearden, 2018) exemplifies such concern. Russia has been labelled one of the most pervasive countries for corruption in the world (Scheifer & Vishny, 1993, pp. 599–617). Yet, between the period of 2008–2012 Russia was noted 'the top nationality in terms of application for the visa' (Nathan, Rolfe, & Vargas-Silva, 2013). Furthermore, according to research by *Transparency International* of the 3,352 visas issued between 2008 and 2016, (MAC) (2018) 706 (21.06 per cent) were issued to Russians. Although it is true 'the UK has continued to build economic ties with Russia' what is crucial, is that this will only continue to persist 'assuming […] business interests can be isolated from a political relationship that has become more and more confrontational' (Allan, 2018). Yet, it seems the isolation of such pivotal spheres has not been possible, given the Tier 1 (Investor) visa's facilitation of the Salisbury Novichok attacks in March and June 2018 (Sandal, 2012). This was thanks to the distribution of the visa being grounded upon a total lack of due diligence; facilitating Russian Kremlin Intelligence residency, and thus the investment of illicit capital (Sengupta, 2018). As Sengupta (2018) states, 'after the Salisbury attack there was much publicity about the British government enforcing "Unexplained Wealth Orders" ' (UWO), enabling the investigation of assets by the Home Office. Following the attack, Theresa May stated,

> it is right that we look generally to see whether this is a part of our visa regime that is being used properly or whether there are loopholes in it for people to be able to use it as access to the UK when otherwise we would not be granting them access. (Liaison Committee, Oral evidence, 2018)

It seems May even admits the existence of such an exceptional commodity, grants permission for the system to be abused. Moreover, whilst applications for the visa 'have already fallen since 2015, when candidates were asked to provide more information about their wealth' (Sandal, 2012), one should not overlook that this Kremlin attack occurred in 2018. Hence, it seems further emphasis on UWO's, as former Home Secretary Amber Rudd suggested, is not a sufficient method of protecting the UK from further attacks. Additionally, such a retrospective response does not ameliorate the fact the visa simplified Russia's ability to cause a fatality and seriously injure three other British Citizens within the UK.

4.2. UWO and the Abylazov Fraud...

Additionally, the present lack of proper enforcement of UWO's is evidenced in the case of *JSC BTA Bank* v. *Ablyazov.*[23] Mr Abylazov was the chairman of the BTA Bank, however, the bank was being probed by regulators who had found almost 20% of its loan portfolio to be 'non-performing'. It was thus suspected that Mr Abylazov had perpetrated a huge and systematic fraud against BTA, by purporting to lend or otherwise transfer billions of dollars to offshore companies with no assets, which appeared to be in the control of Abylazov or his associates. Thereby, BTA brought Court proceedings requiring him to disclose his assets. For completeness, the judgement of the court led to Mr Abylazov being sentenced to time in jail for contempt of court due to his refusal to abide by the requirement to disclose assets. Yet, what is crucial is that Mr Abylazov's son, ancillary to the time of Mr Abylazov's fraud to BTA, had applied and been awarded a Tier 1 (Investor) Visa, through the investment of £1 million which had been provided to Madiyar by his father (Pegg, 2017). It is very likely that such funding from Mr Abylazov – a criminal who has been 'accused of one of the world's biggest frauds' (Neate, 2012) – stemmed from fraudulent funds. This draws the obvious conclusion, that the visa can hardly be characterised a marker of 'good character and civic competence' (Sandal, 2012). Instead, we see the commodification of the migration system attracting corrupt individuals and their dependants to secure their residency, 'thereby receiving an implicit endorsement of their money's legitimacy from the UK' (Transparency International UK Report, 2016).

Further, the *Abylazov Fraud* only represents one possible case of illicit funds being invested in the UK in exchange for the Tier 1 (Investor) Visa. The 'blind-faith period' spanning from 2008 to April 2015, was a period within which 'there was no necessity for individuals to obtain a UK bank account before applying and being awarded a Tier 1 (Investor) visa' (Transparency International UK Report, 2016). This period provided a 'huge loophole that allowed visas to be granted without any checks being carried out' (Transparency International UK Report, 2016). The exploitation of this 'loophole' is evident given '97 per cent of all investors using the scheme' from 2008 to 2016 'invested their money' during this period (Transparency International UK Report, 2016). Whilst it is true that criminal records are a ground for refusal of the visa under Part 9 of the Immigration Rules,[24] this will have 'no effect on individuals involved in grand corruption where the highest levels of government are complicit and where no prior conviction may exist'.[25] Hence due diligence in this respect is not satisfactory and has never been satisfactory enough to provide a clearly transparent transaction. As a result, not only has residency in the UK been placed on the market, it is problematically being offered for sale with no proper infrastructure so as to prevent corrupt and illicit individuals and funds entering the UK.

5. PART IV: THE DEGRADATION OF SOCIETAL NORMS AND VALUES

The visa is also responsible for undermining the sacredness of migration; affirming inequality underpins a migrant's chance of success in the system and highlighting and promoting hierarchical values in society in relation to the possession of wealth.

5.1. An (Un)ethical Market?

It must not be forgotten 'the most important ideal that the modern market attempts to embody is a particular conception of freedom'. (TANASOCA) (2016) Every human has the 'choice and consumption of commodities in private life'. (TANASOCA) (2016) Yet, to apply this market logic of 'choice and consumption' to the purchase of residency, seems somewhat fuelled by a form of idiosyncrasy.

It is true that the Tier 1 (Investor) Visa, 'does not compromise a person's bodily integrity, it does not breach taboos or clear social norms'. (Perrott & Yu, 2018) To adopt Anderson's analogy: it is not the prostitution of one's body for sexual gratification. Nevertheless, the Tier 1 (Investor) visa is the effective lease of residency for money, that is, assuming no application for ILR is made. Whether such practice be a form of prostitution by the government is something for the reader of this chapter to decide .... Yet for assistance,

> in today's age of globalisation and privatisation, full membership in the political community remains the only good that even the mightiest economic conglomerate cannot offer to the skilled migrant. Only governments can allocate the legal status [...] to those not born as members (Sandal, 2012).

However, the visa to some extent bypasses any good in the government's ability to transfer such a status, (Perrott & Yu, 2018) resultantly undermining the sacredness of the migration system in exchange for monetary gain. Again, as aforementioned, the visa does not offer an exclusive right to citizenship. However, the existence of accelerated ILR as a reward to those who invest over £5 or £10 million under the programme does not lack significance. Many academics have alluded to the boundary between ILR and citizenship status being 'blurred' (Lord Goldsmith, 2008, p. 76) and encompassing a 'long-standing fuzziness' (Clayton, 2014). Some, such as Spiro (2008), even go as far as to allege 'the real prize is legal residency, not citizenship' (p. 159). It seems the line between each status is undoubtedly obscure, and the common law has not led to any clarification. Cases such as *Al-Rawi* v. *SSHD* (Sandal, 2012), and *R (on the application of Abbassi)* v. *Secretary of State for Foreign and Commonwealth Affairs*,[26] are illustrative of an outright contradiction regarding what ILR status actually requires of the migrant's country of residence. Each of these cases questions whether the UK had the right to intervene with another state on behalf of an individual holding UK ILR status. The Court held in the former that the UK was able to intervene, whereas in the latter it was held the Court did not have the power to compel the government to intervene in any particular way. Accordingly, with a conceptually blurred line between ILR and citizenship status, it seems the possession of money has circumvented the sacredness that traditionally conceptualised permanent membership – with a simple transaction adept in acquiring ILR.

5.2. Equality (or Lack, Thereof)?

Furthermore, the overwhelming sense of inequality which results from the existence of the visa should not be overlooked. As Boatca˘ (2014) notes, 'time and again, canonical sociology has presented and analysed citizenship as a counterbalance of social inequalities' (Wallerstein, Chase-Dunn, & Suter, 2014, pp. 3–18). From Weber through Parsons and up to Turner (1993), the 'institutionalization of citizenship' (Delanty, 1997, pp. 285–303) was seen as part of a sequence of social change characteristic of the West. This entailed a progression from bondage to freedom and from ascribed to achieved positions in the inequality structure, ultimately transitioning from tradition to modernity. Yet citizenship, being far from reasonably easily accessible, has meant the growth of visa programmes has been a key in the decline of 'space and territorial boundaries'.[27] In turn this has helped to promote the erosion of the model of the 'state container' (Beck, 2008) all in the pursuit of an equal foundation for all humans to enter and reside in a country. However, the Tier 1 (Investor) Visa disregards any definition of equality. It instead offers those classed as high-net-worth individuals a considerably greater chance of being granted a visa due to the exceptions and 'loopholes' it provides in the pursuit of residency.

Moreover, as aforesaid the increase from £1 million to £2 million in the minimum investment requirement has exacerbated the disparity induced by the programme. It is now evident that there is an exceptionally abundant financial gap between the majority of UK citizens in comparison to applicants for the investor programme. For example, in the UK the median household disposable income was £26,400 in 2015/16 (Office for National Statistics), where conversely investors possessing a visa must possess a minimum of £2 million in disposable income. Hence, the gap between citizens and investors has quite evidently broadened. Subsequently, not only are investors to a larger extent more financially stable they are also given the upper-hand in the manipulation of the migration system through the facilitation of their wealth.

5.3. The Hierarchy

As a consequence of such inequality the commodification of the migration system has highlighted the continued and prevalent existence of hierarchical values in society. By offering such a programme the government has instilled the societal value that wealth makes an individual the most desirable migrant candidate. To the extent that academics, such as Shachar and Hirschl, have labelled investor migrants the governments 'prized assets'. (Shachar & Hirschl, 2014, pp. 231–257). It is thus cogent, that the existence of the visa has the potential to encourage states to be more reluctant to grant residency to refugees, and more inclined to grant it to rich investors. (TANASOCA) (2018) This epitomises the existence of the UK's hierarchy of desired migrants, with those possessing excessive financial affluence recognised as top ranking, where ostensibly refugees and migrants with little financial backing perhaps even fearing prosecution, conflict and generalised violences are placed at the bottom. As a result of this indisputable pursuit for money, the government has neglected the 'dignity' of numerous individuals – a quality which should be 'above price' (Kant, 1785).

To the contrary Hidalgo (2016) argues that, if states can legitimately impose restrictions on access, deciding who can or cannot join the community, then states can also legitimately put a price on restriction (pp. 223–239). Yet, if such logic were plausible, then by analogy it follows that universities, who can legitimately impose restrictions on access to their courses, could also legitimately put a price on access. Such a suggestion can only be conceptualised as draconian, yet regrettably Hidalgo's logic is the rationale we see the government imparting on society. The result is an emphasis on hierarchical positions of wealth in relation to a person's status in society.

6. CONCLUSION

International migration has been transformed into a 'global business' (Sørensen, 2012). The existence of an outright payment for residency visa scheme has commodified the UK's migration system. This 'business' (Sørensen, 2012) comprises not only of just a migratory market, but also encompasses 'private lawyers, travel agents, recruiters and brokers' (Sørensen, 2012) as well as many more indirectly linked spheres of work. Each aiding investors to bypass normal legal migratory requirements to the UK's detriment and the Investors benefit. Yet, despite the visa's eminence, the government has consistently failed to regulate the Tier 1 (Investor) visa effectively. Instead they have shown a willingness to grant a blind eye in relation to the origins of finances being invested, seeming to lack any motivation to effectively regulate UWO's. It seems the government's persistent talk of investigating 'whether the visa regime' 'is being used properly'[28] as most recently advocated by Ms May, is an example of the government living up to the idiom 'all talk and no action'. As a result, we see the development of controversial societal values, namely inequality and the affirmation of a hierarchy of desired migrants. Furthermore, despite the government pledges to keep the UK safe from harm, we see the visa facilitating acts of terror. Consequently, it is contended that the Tier 1 (Investor) visa should be revoked. In the alternative, the visa should be frozen from operation until effective stringent due diligence checks have been put in place. However, ultimately it should not be overlooked that as of yet, the UK's migration system remains a commodity available exclusively to the rich – a golden ticket ready and waiting.

NOTES

1. Immigration Rules, para. 245EE(e).
2. *ibid.*
3. *ibid.*
4. *ibid.*, para 245EE(c)(i).

5. *ibid.*, para. 54 to 65-SD Appendix A.
6. *ibid.*, para 245ED(a).
7. *ibid.*, para 245EB.
8. Table 9B: 'Applications for indefinite leave to remain from applicants who initially applied to enter the category before 6 November 2014 as referred to in paragraph 57(b)', see parts 1 and 3 of the Table. Retrieved from https://www.gov.uk/guidance/immigration-rules/immigration-rules-appendix-a-attributes
9. n. 1., para. 245HB and see the guidance in paragraphs 80-80E of 'Tier 2 (General) Limit' section. Retrieved from https://www.gov.uk/guidance/immigration-rules/immigration-rules-appendix-a-attributes
10. n. 1, para. 245HF(c)(ii)(2),(3) and (4).
11. n. 1, Appendix KoLL, Knowledge of Language and Life.
12. n.3., para. 245HH.
13. n.1., para 36, part 1.
14. n. 1., para. 245HB(q), (r).
15. Visa tables volume 1, section vi_04. Retrieved from https://www.gov.uk/government/publications/immigration-statistics-january-to-march-2017/why-do-people-come-to-the-uk-2-to-work
16. Visa tables volume 1, section vi_04. Retrieved from https://www.gov.uk/government/publications/immigration-statistics-january-to-march-2017/why-do-people-come-to-the-uk-2-to-work
17. Section (3)(2), The Freedom of Information and Data Protection (Appropriate Limit and Fees) Regulation 2004.
18. n. 1.
19. Article 20, Treaty on the Functioning of the European Union (TFEU).
20. Grzelczyk, Case C-184/99.
21. n. 38, Article 20(20(a)).
22. n. 1., para. 245(EE)(e).
23. *[2017] EWCA Civ 40.*
24. n. 1, Part 9, 2(b) and (c).
25. Section 4.1, Transparency International UK Report (2015).
26. [2006] EWCA Civ 1279.
27. [2003] UKHRR 76.
28. Liaison Committee, Oral evidence: The Prime Minister, HC 905, Tuesday 27 March 2018 (Ordered by the House of Commons to be published on 27 March 2018), see Question 6. Retrieved from https://www.parliament.uk/documents/commons-committees/liaison/LC-27-03-18.pdf

Bibliography

Anderson, E. (1990). The ethical limitations of the market. *Economics and Philosophy*, *6*(2).

Beck, U. (2008). The cosmopolitan perspective: sociology of the second age of modernity*.*British Journal of Sociology*, *51*(1).

Clayton, G. (2014). *Immigration and Asylum Law*. Oxford: Oxford University Press.

Delanty, G. (1997). Models of citizenship: Defining European identity of citizenship. *Journal of Citizenship Studies*, *1*(3).

Hidalgo, J. (2016). Selling citizenship: A defence.*Journal of Applied Philosophy*, *33*(3), 223–239.

Joppke, C. (2010). The inevitable lightening of citizenship.*European Journal of Sociology, Chicago, Illinois*.

Kant, I. (1785). *Groundwork of the metaphysics of morals*. (G. Mary, Trans. ed.). New York, NY: Cambridge University Press.

Keister, A. (2014). The one percent. *Annual Review of Sociology*, *40*, 347–367.

Mayes, C. (1957). The sale of Peerages in Early Stuart England. *Journal of Modern History*, *29*(1).

Prahbhat, D. (2018). *Britishness, belonging and citizenship: Experiencing nationality law*. Bristol: Policy Press.

Rodgers, P. (1997). Changes at the Bank of England.*Quarterly Bulletin*, *37*(3).
Sandal, M. (2012). *What money can't buy: The moral limits of markets*. New York, NY: Farrar, Straus and Girous.
Scheifer, A., & Vishny, R. (1993). Corruption.*The Quarterly Journal of Economics*, *108*(2), 1.
Shachar, A., & Hirschl, R. (2014). On citizenship, states and markets.*Journal of Political Philosophy*, *22*(2).
Sørensen, N. (2012). Revisiting the migration–development nexus: From social networks and remittances to markets for migration control.*International Migration Journal*, *50*(3).
Spiro, P. (2008). *Beyond citizenship: American identity after globalization*. New York, NY: Oxford University Press.
Stein, J. (1995). Prices and trading volume in the housing market: A model with down payment effects. *Quarterly Journal of Economics*, *110*.
Tanasoca, A. (2016). Citizenship for sale: Neomedieval, not just neoliberal?*European Journal of Sociology*, *57*(1).
Turner, B. (1993). *Citizenship and social theory*. London: Sage Publications.
Wallerstein, I., Chase-Dunn, C., & Suter, C. (2014). *Overcoming global inequalities*. London: Routledge, Taylor & Francis Group.

Legislation [Database]

British Nationality Act 1981.
Freedom of Information Act 2000.
Immigration Rules.
The Freedom of Information and Data Protection (Appropriate Limit and Fees) Regulations 2004.

Treaties

Treaty on the Functioning of the European Union.

Jurisprudence

Al-Rawi v. SSHD [2006] EWCA Civ 1279.
Grzelczyk Case C-184/99.
JSC BTA Bank v. *Ablyazov (No 14)* [2017] EWCA Civ 40.
R (on the application of Abbassi) v. *Secretary of State for Foreign and Commonwealth Affairs* [2003] UKHRR 76.

Online Articles and Reports

Allan, D. (2018, October). Managed confrontation UK policy towards Russia after the Salisbury Attack, Russia and Eurasia Programme. *Chatham House*. Retrieved from https://www.chathamhouse.org/publication/managed-confrontation-uk-policy-towards-russia-after-salisbury-attack
Aston, B. (2011). Bonds: What are gilts? Investors chronicle. *Investors Chronicle*, December 6.
BBC News. (2018, December). Investor Visa halted in money laundering crackdown. Retrieved from https://www.bbc.co.uk/news/uk-46463319
Dearden, L. (2018). 'Golden visas' allowing Russian and Chinese investors to settle in UK suspended over money laundering.*The Independent*, December. Retrieved from https://www.independent.co.uk/news/uk/home-news/investor-visas-tier-one-uk-suspended-money-laundering-financial-crime-immigration-russia-china-a8670876.html
Helm, T. (2014, February). Stop rich overseas investors from buying up UK homes, report urges.*The Guardian*.

Lord Goldsmith, Q. C. (2008). *Citizenship: Our common bond*. London: Ministry of Justice, Citizenship Review. Retrieved from http://image.guardian.co.uk/sys-files/Politics/documents/2008/03/11/citizenship-report-full.pdf

Liaison Committee, Oral evidence. (2018, March). The Prime Minister, HC 905 (Ordered by the House of Commons to be published on 27 March 2018), see Question 6. Retrieved from https://www.parliament.uk/documents/commons-committees/liaison/LC-27-03-18.pdf

Migration Advisory Committee (MAC). (2014). Tier 1 (investor) route: Investment thresholds and economic benefits. Retrieved from https://www.gov.uk/government/publications/the-investment-limits-and-economic-benefits-of-the-tier-1-investor-route-feb-2014

Migration Advisory Committee (MAC). (2018). Responses to the MAC consultation on the Tier 1 Investor Route [FOI]. Retrieved from https://www.gov.uk/government/publications/tier-1-investor-call-for-evidence-responses

Nathan, M., Rolfe, H., & Vargas-Silva, C. (2013, June). *The economic and labour market impacts of Tier 1 entrepreneur and investor migrants*. Oxford: National Institute of Economic and Social Research, The Migration Observatory at the University of Oxford.

Neate, R. (2012). Arrest warrant for Kazakh billionaire accused of one of world's biggest frauds. *The Guardian*, February.

Office for National Statistics. Retrieved from https://www.ons.gov.uk/peoplepopulationandcommunity/personalandhouseholdfinances/incomeandwealth/bulletins/nowcastinghouseholdincomeintheuk/2015to2016#trends-in-household-incomes

Pegg, D. (2017). The 'golden visa' deal: 'We have in effect been selling off British citizenship to the rich'. *The Guardian*, July. Retrieved from https://www.theguardian.com/uk-news/2017/jul/04/golden-visa-immigration-deal-british-citizenship-home-office

Perrott, J., & Yu, J. (2018, November). Tier 1 (investor) visa, (Macfarlanes). Retrieved from https://www.macfarlanes.com/what-we-think/in-depth/2018/tier-1-investor-visa/

Rankin, J. (2018). Super-rich passport schemes open door to criminals, activists say. *The Independent*, October.

Sengupta, K. (2018). UK's weak response on Litvinenko murder encouraged Russia to carry out Salisbury attack, new report claims. *The Independent*, October.

Transparency International UK Report. (2015, October). Gold Rush: Investment visas and corrupt capital flows into the UK. Retrieved from http://www.transparency.org.uk/publications/gold-rush-investment-visas-and-corrupt-capital-flows-into-the-uk/

Transparency International UK Report. (2016). Paradise lost: Ending the UK's role as a safe haven for corrupt individuals, their allies and assets.*Recommendation 8*, April. Retrieved from http://www.transparency.org.uk/publications/paradise-lost/

Tryfonidou, A. (2017). *Investment residence in the UK: Past and future*. Investment Migration Policy Briefs, IMC-PB 2017/1. Retrieved from http://centaur.reading.ac.uk/69288/1/Tryfonidou%20IMC%20PB1%202017.pdf

United Kingdom Debt Management Office. Gilt market data. Retrieved from https://www.dmo.gov.uk/data/gilt-market/

William, A. (2018). Overseas buyers snap up majority of exclusive London homes.*Financial Times London*, February.

Other Sources

Becker, G., & Becker, G. N. (1998). *The economics life: From Baseball to affirmative action to immigration, how real-world issues affect our everyday life*. New York, NY: McGrawe Hill.

Boatcă, M. (2014). Commodification of Citizenship, Global Inequalities and the Modern Transmission of Property.

Borna, S., & Stearns, J. (2002). The ethics and efficacy of selling national citizenship. *Journal of Business Ethics*, *37*(2).

Friedman, M., & Friedman, R. (1980). *Free to choose*. London: Harmondsmith, Penguin.

Glick Schiller, N., & Faist, T. (2010). *Migration, development and transnationalization: A critical stance*. New York, NY: Berghahn Books.

Goodhart, D. (2006). *Progressive nationalism: Citizenship and the Left*. London: Demos.

Hall, P., & Soskice, D. (2001). *Varieties of capitalism. The institutional foundations of comparative advantage*. Oxford: Oxford University Press.

Hicks, J. (1939). *Value & Capital*. Oxford: Clarendon Press.

Jordan, B., & Düvell, F. (2003). *Migration: The boundaries of equality and justice*. Cambridge: Polity Press.

Jorgenson, D. (1967). *Determinants of investment behavior*. New York, NY: Columbia University Press.

Menz, G. (2008). *The political economy of managed migration: Non-state actors, Europeanization, and the politics of designing migration policies*. Oxford: Oxford University Press.

Rudolph, C. (2003). Security and the political economy of international migration. *American Political Science Review*, *97*(4).

Sahlins, M. (1972). *Stone Age economic*. New York, NY: Aldine.

Satz, D. (2010). *Why some things should not be for sale: The moral limits of markets*. New York, NY: Oxford University Press.

Tobin, J. (1970). On limiting the domain of inequality. *Journal of Law and Economics*, *1*(7).

Walzer, M. (1983). *Spheres of Justice: A defence of pluralism and equality*. Oxford: Robertson.

Wellman, C., & Cole, P. (2011). *Debating the ethics of immigration: Is there a right to exclude?*Oxford: Oxford University Press.

Printed and bound by CPI Group (UK) Ltd, Croydon, CR0 4YY

28/05/2025

14678151-0001